St. Catharines Ontario Book 1 in Colour Photos, Saving Our History One Photo at a Time

Photography
by Barbara Raué
2018

Series Name:
Cruising Ontario

Book 189: St. Catharines Book 1

Cover photo: 109 Main Street, Page 23

Series Name: Cruising Ontario
Saving Our History One Photo at a Time in colour photos

Books Available in Alphabetical Order:
Aberfoyle, Acton, Alton, Amherstburg, Ancaster, Arthur, Aylmer, Ayr, Bloomingdale, Brantford, Burlington, Caledon, Caledonia, Cambridge, Clifford, Conestogo, Delhi, Dorchester to Aylmer, Drayton, Drumbo, Dundas, Eden Mills, Elmira, Elora, Essex, Fergus, Guelph, Hagersville, Hamilton, Hanover, Harriston, Hespeler, Jarvis, Kingston, Kingsville, Kitchener, Linwood, Listowel, London, Lucknow, Mono, Mount Forest, Neustadt, New Hamburg, Niagara-on-the-Lake, Oakville, Orangeville, Orillia, Owen Sound, Palmerston, Peterborough, Petrolia, Port Elgin, Preston, Rockwood, Sarnia, Seaforth, Sheffield, Shelburne, Simcoe, Southampton, St. Jacobs, St. Marys, St. Thomas, Stoney Creek, Stratford, Thamesford, Tillsonburg, Waterdown, Waterford, Waterloo, Welland, Wellesley, Windsor, Wingham, Woodstock

Book 157: Brockville
Book 158: Merrickville
Book 159: Smiths Falls
Book 160: Portland, Newboro
Book 161: Westport & Area
Book 162: Perth
Book 163-166: Belleville
Book 167-168: Port Colborne
Book 169: Erin in Colour
Book 170: Goderich in Colour
Book 171: Sault Ste. Marie
Book 172: Lake Superior
Book 173-176: Thunder Bay
Book 177-179: Paris
Book 180-181: St. George
Book 182-183: Burford
Book 184: Mt Pleasant, Onondaga, Newport
Book 185-186: Grimsby
Book 187: Toronto in Colour
Book 188: Collingwood Colour
Book 189-193: St. Catharines

Other Books by Barbara Raue

Coins of Gold

Arrows, Indians and Love

The Life and Times of Barbara
Volume 1: Inventions That Have Enhanced My Life
Volume 2: Entertainment That I Have Enjoyed
Volume 3: East Coast Trips
Volume 4: Olympics Have Always Intrigued Me
Volume 5: Wonders of the World
Volume 6: Caribbean Cruises We Have Enjoyed
Volume 7: Animals
Volume 8: Storms and Other Major Disasters in My Lifetime
Volume 9: Wars, Terrorist Attacks and Major Disasters

The Cromwell Family Book

Laura Secord Discovered

Daddy Where Are You?

Montana Series
Book 1: Montana Dream
Book 2: Life on the Montana Frontier
Book 3: Montana to Boston and Back
Book 4: Montana Sons Go to War
Book 5: Montana Sons Return From War

Visit Barbara's website to view all of her books
http://barbararaue.ca

Table of Contents

Port Dalhousie

    Main Street — Page 7

    Lakeport Road — Page 41

    Hogan's Alley — Page 49

    Canal Street — Page 51

    Lock Street — Page 61

Architectural Terms — Page 67

Building Styles — Page 69

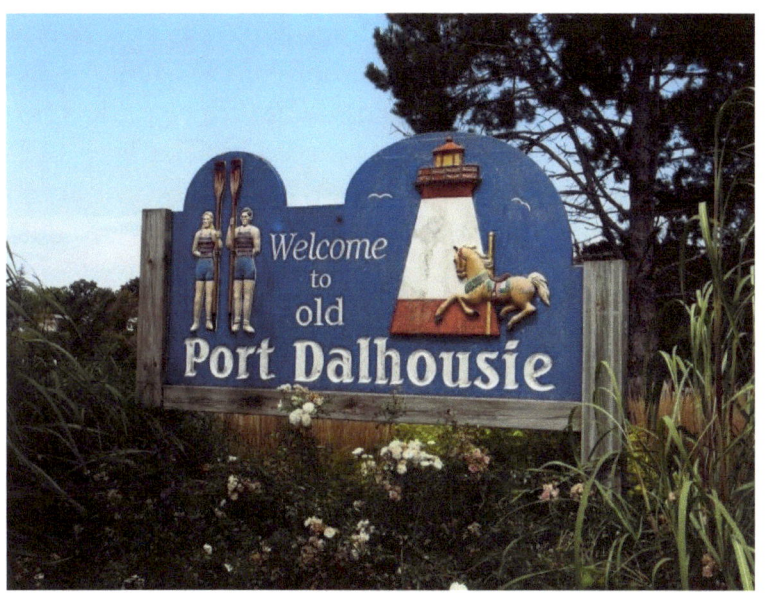

      The Port Dalhousie community is located on a small peninsula that separates Martindale Pond from Lake Ontario. The historical growth of this community around an elongated road grid pattern can be directly attributed to the development of the Welland canals, commerce, industry and Great Lakes shipping during the 19th century. By the end of the 20th century, Port Dalhousie began to be recognized as an area of rich cultural heritage.

      The commercial core, located on Lakeport Road, Lock Street and Hogan´s Alley, is characterized by varying architectural styles from the 19th and early 20th centuries, ranging from red and buff brick to Italianate.

      The residential area is comprised of dwellings once inhabited by sailors, canal workers, business people, lock tenders, farmers and many other individuals from an eclectic mix of social classes. Architectural styles include Gothic Revival, Colonial Revival, and Neo-classical among others.

Port Dalhousie was the terminus for the first three routes of the Welland Canal, built in 1820, 1845 and 1889. The city's most popular beach, on the shore of Lake Ontario, is located in Port Dalhousie at Lakeside Park. The park is home to an antique carousel which was carved by Charles I. D. Looff in 1905 and brought to St. Catharines in 1921. It continues to provide amusement for young and old alike, at just 5 cents a ride. Port Dalhousie is named for George Ramsay, 9th Earl of Dalhousie, Governor General of British North America from 1820-1828.

At the time of European colonization, the British Crown appropriated the land from the Neutral Indians, and transferred title of the area to Captain Peter Tenbroeck, a United Empire Loyalist officer in Butler's Rangers, as part of an 800 acre land grant. Tenbroeck and other settlers established farms along the Twelve Mile Creek. Within a few years, ships began to ply the waters of Lake Ontario, but only small craft could navigate to the fledgling mills and hamlet of Shipman's Corners, later St. Catharines.

The northern entrance to the Welland Canal was at Port Dalhousie. Industries and services to meet the needs of the growing settlement were established. In 1837, a Scottish boat builder called Robert Abbey started a shipyard at Port Dalhousie, building yawls, sailing yachts and eventually steam yachts.

Confederation in 1867 was a major factor in the building of the Third Welland Canal. A new and enlarged waterway was needed for the larger steamers on the Great Lakes. By 1890 almost 300,000 tons of cargo were shipped along the canal each year, primarily wheat, corn, coal and forest products. By 1914, this had increased to almost four million tons. Further canal enlargements were needed and a new Welland Ship Canal was completed in 1930 which bypassed Port Dalhousie.

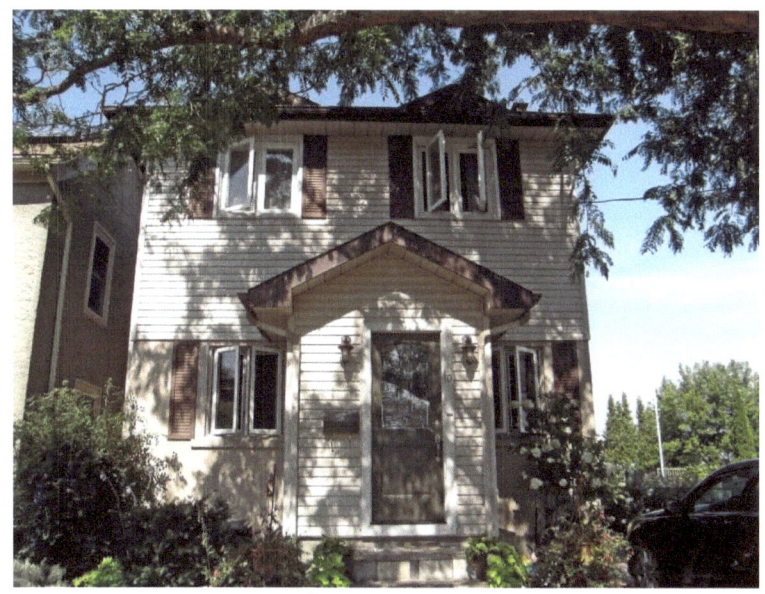

10 Main Street

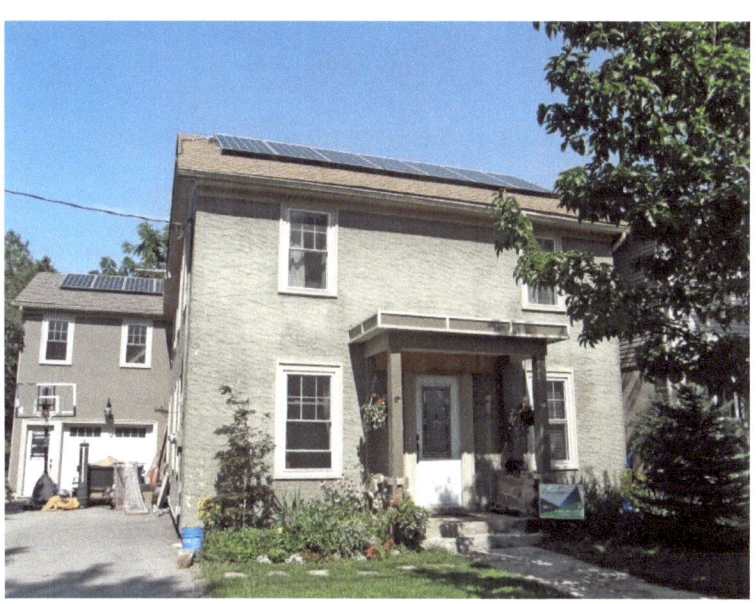

12 Main Street

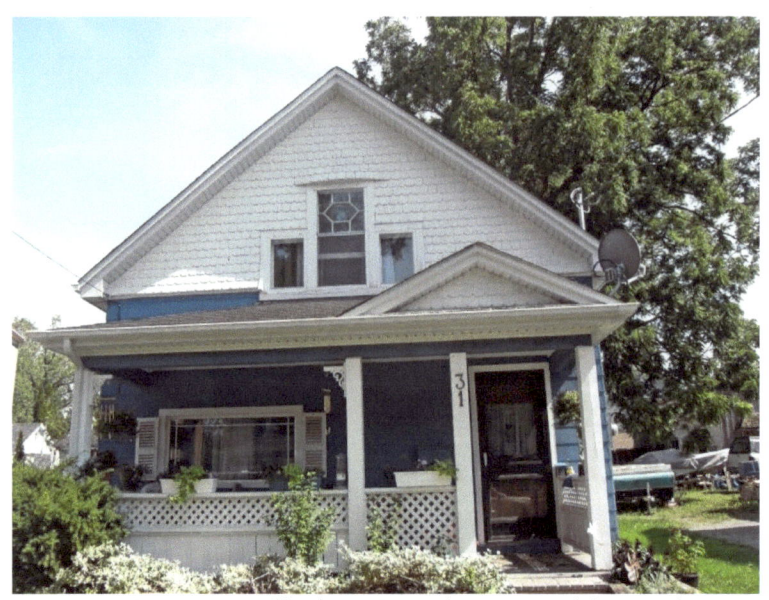

31 Main Street – Palladian Window in gable, pediment

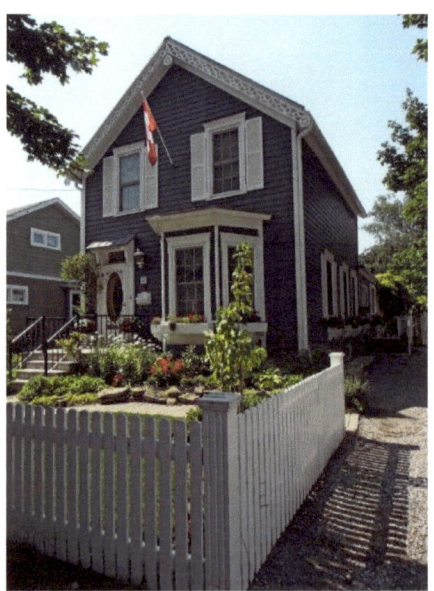

34 Main Street – bay window

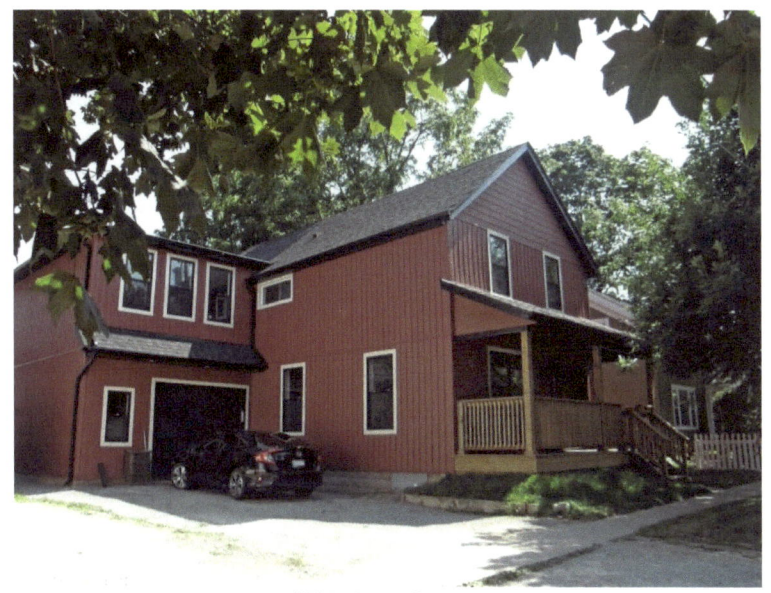

37 Main Street

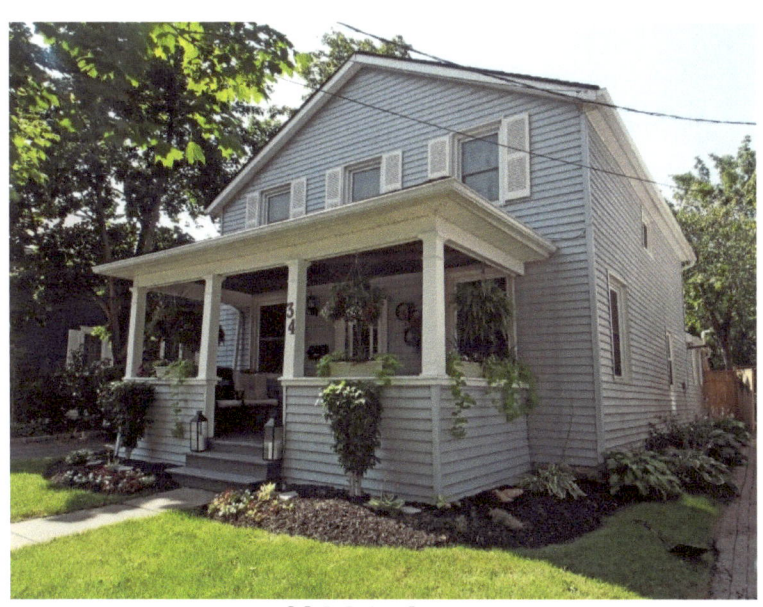

38 Main Street

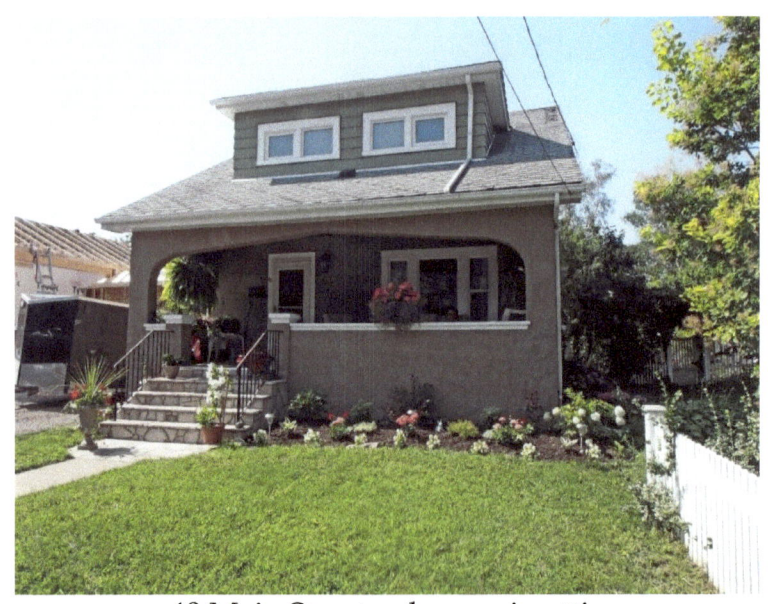
40 Main Street – dormer in attic

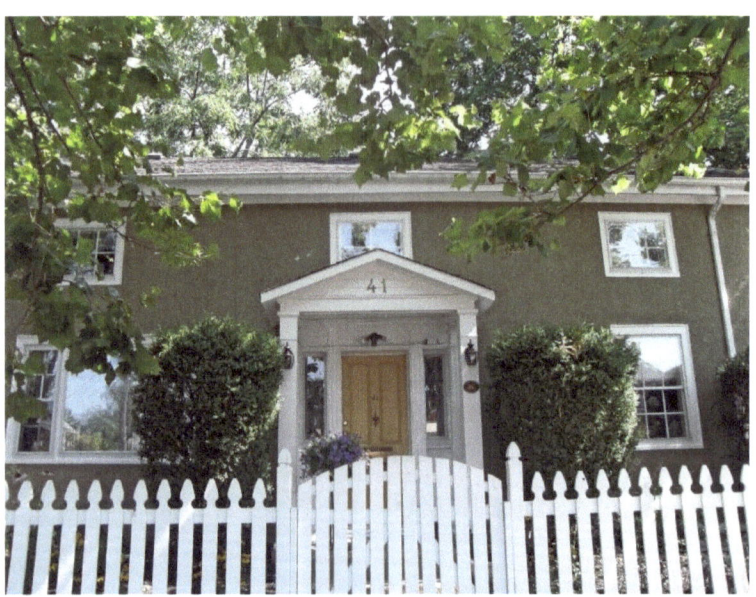
41 Main Street

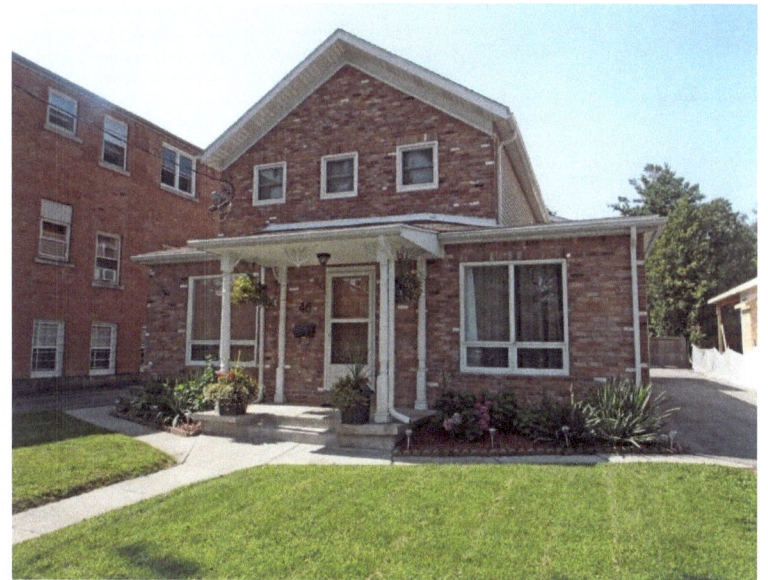

46 Main Street

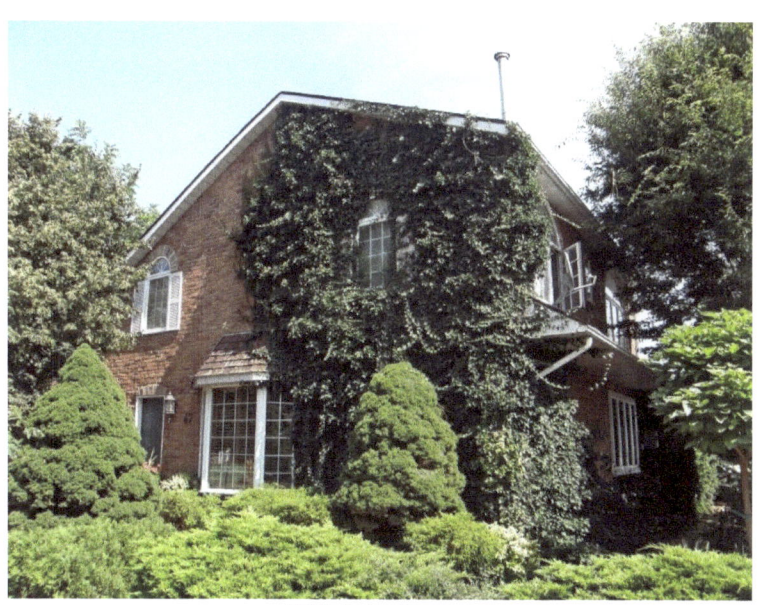

47 Main Street

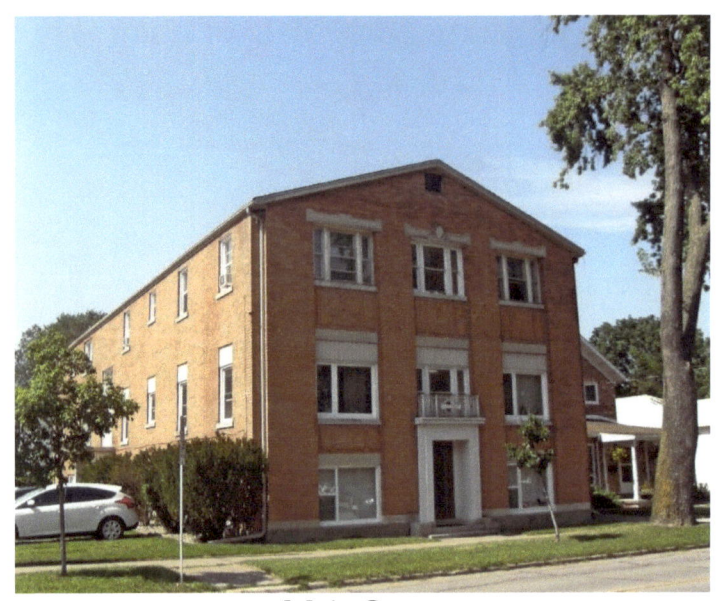

Main Street

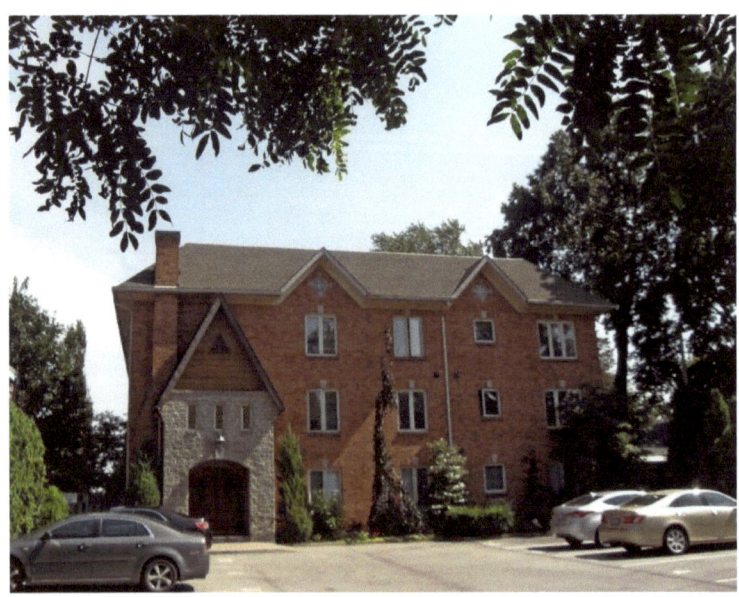

55 Main Street

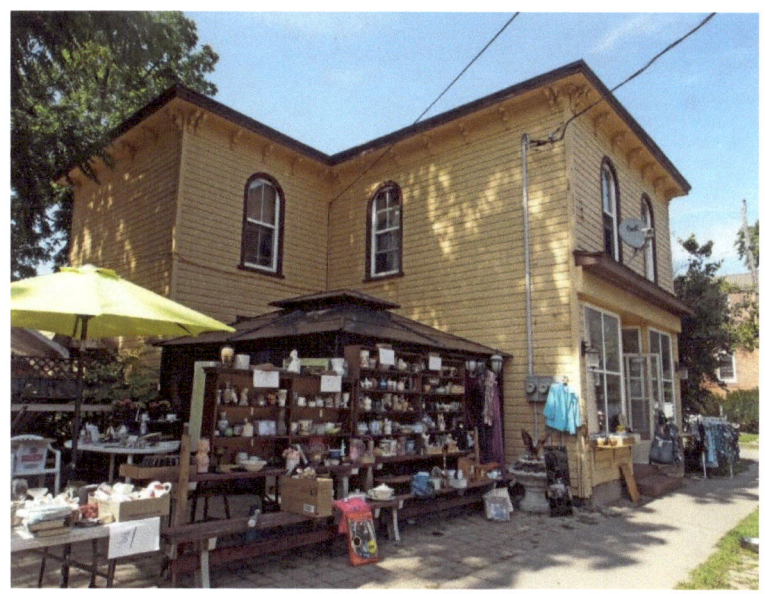

Main Street

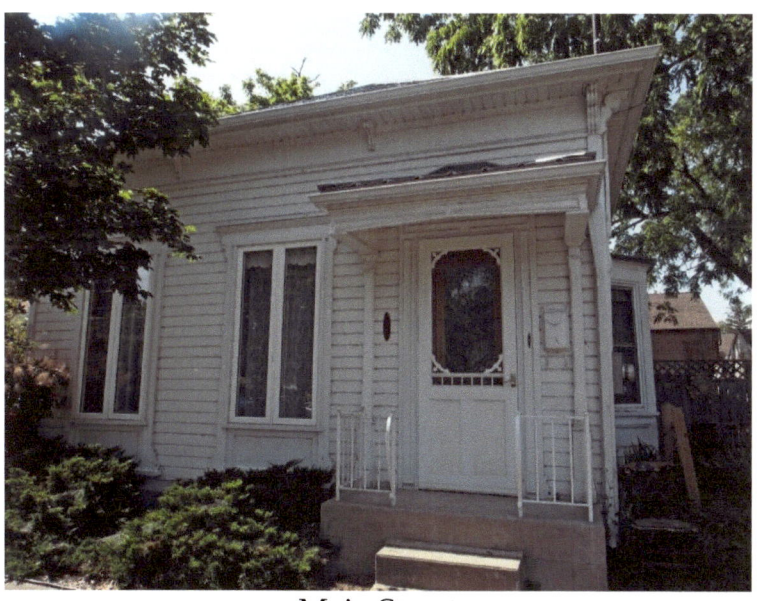

Main Street

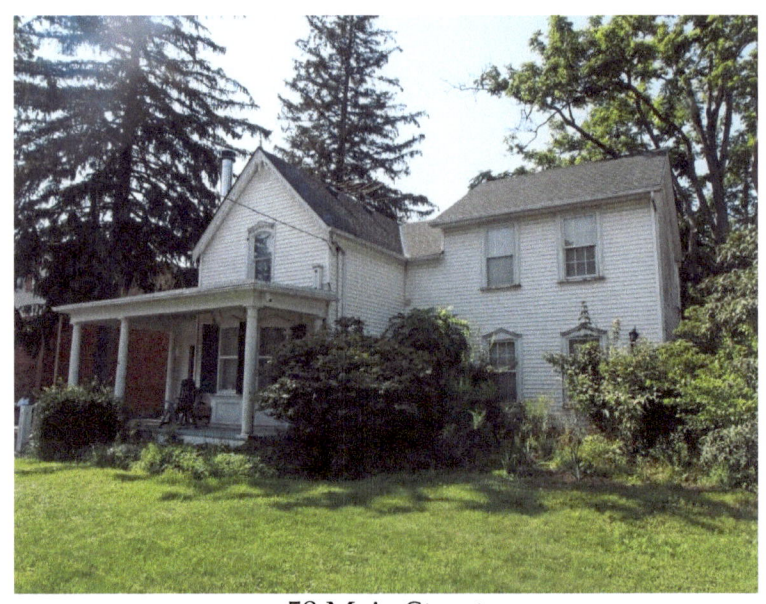

58 Main Street

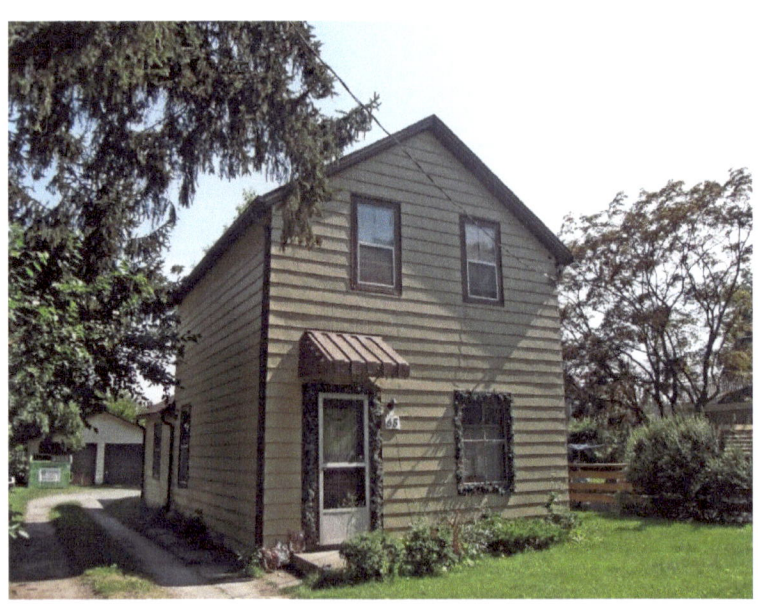

65 Main Street

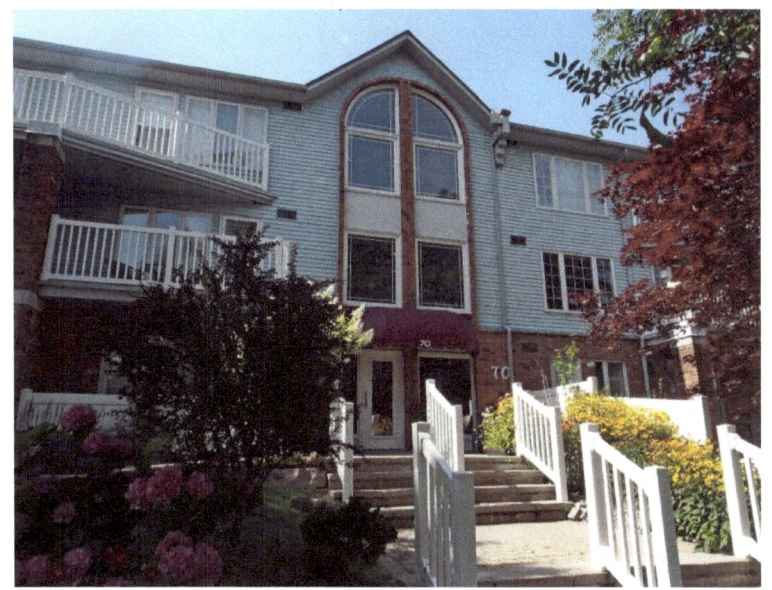

70 Main Street

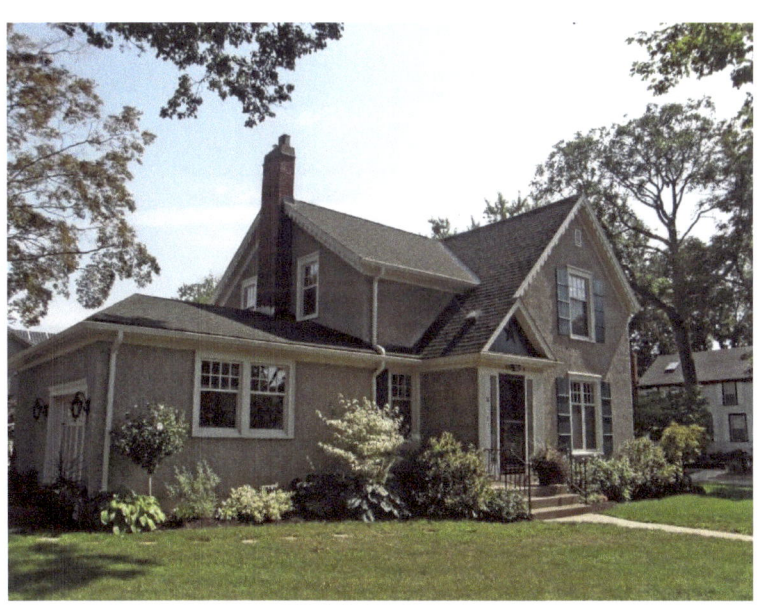

71 Main Street

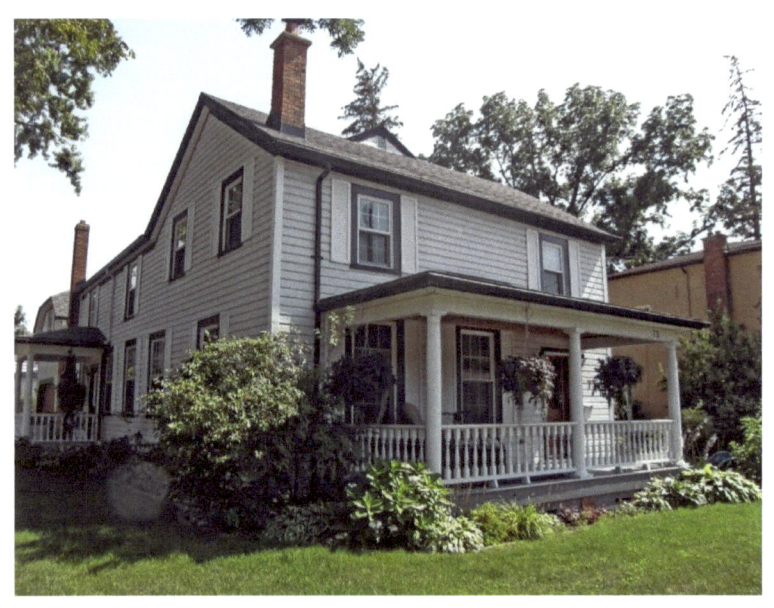

73 Main Street

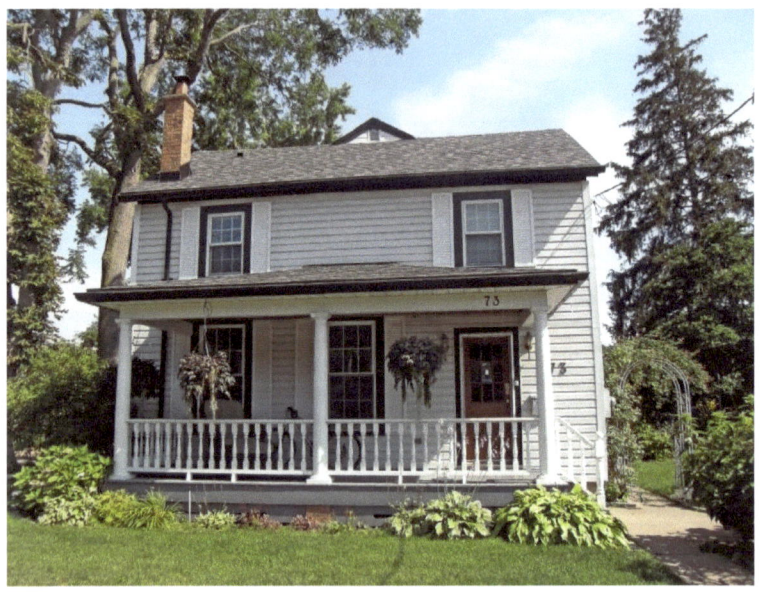

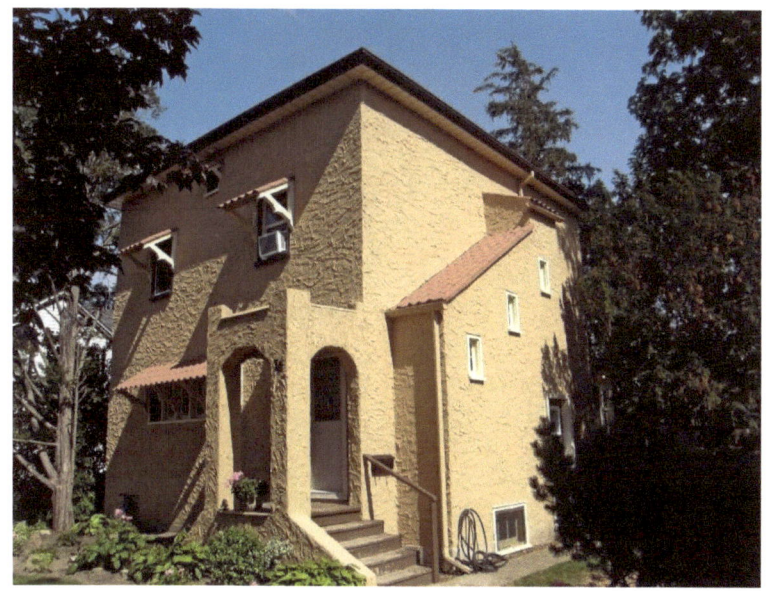

74 Main Street

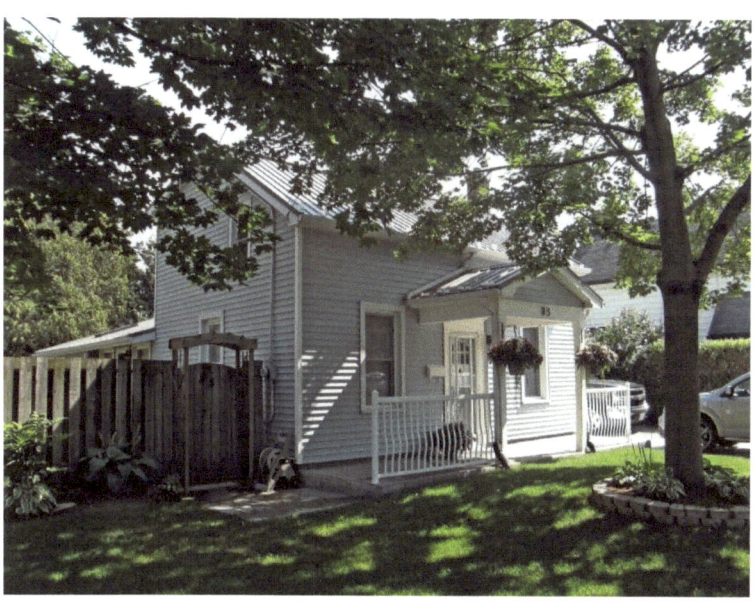

85 Main Street

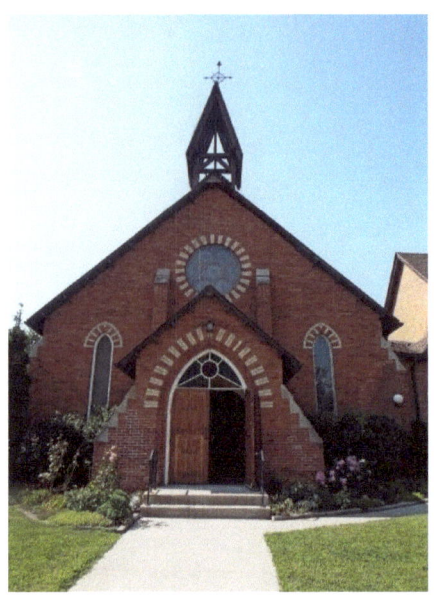

80 Main Street – St. John's Anglican Church – Gothic Revival style - dichromatic brickwork, rose window, lancet windows

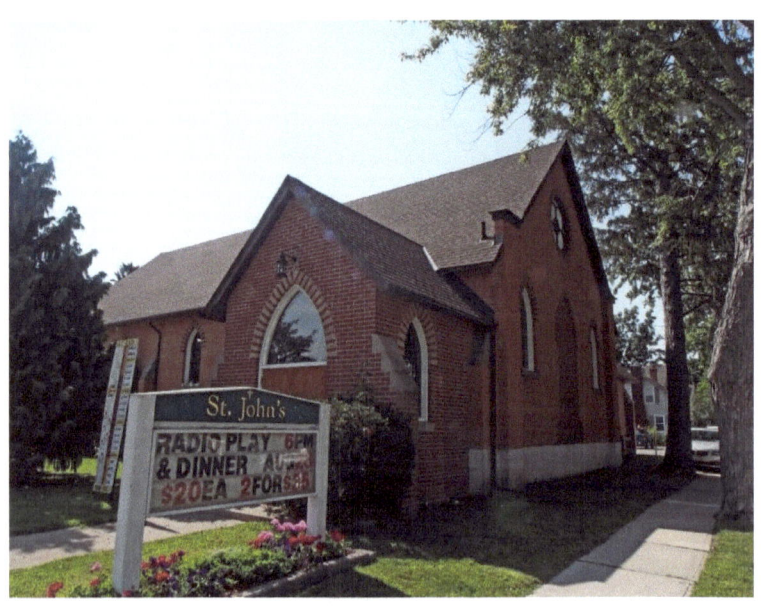

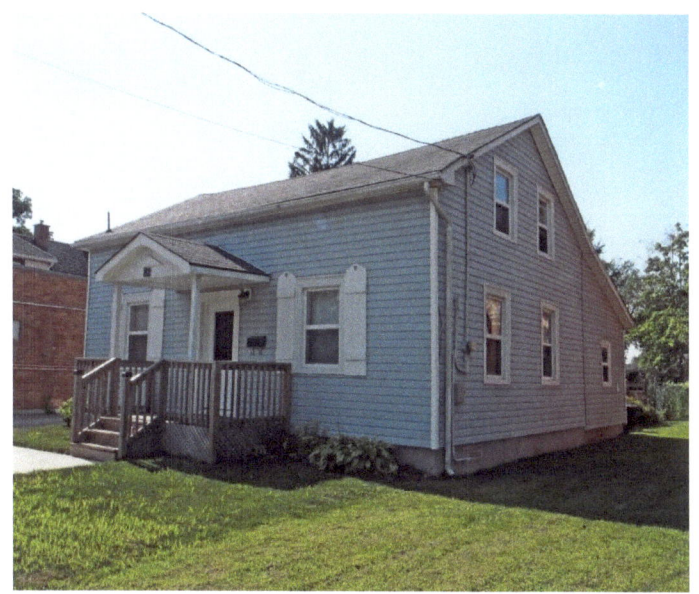

82 Main Street - saltbox

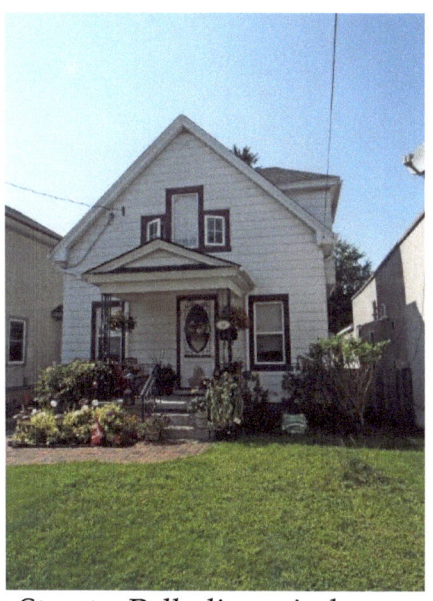

86 Main Street – Palladian window, pediment

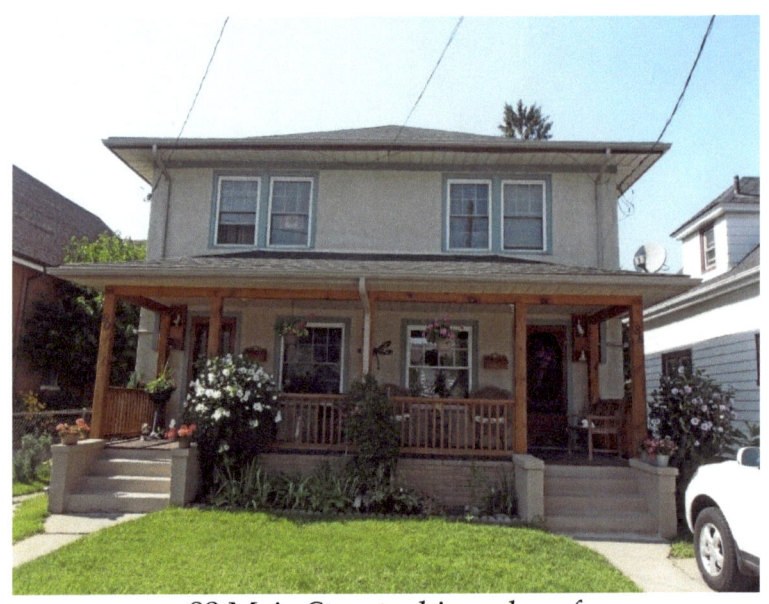

88 Main Street – hipped roof

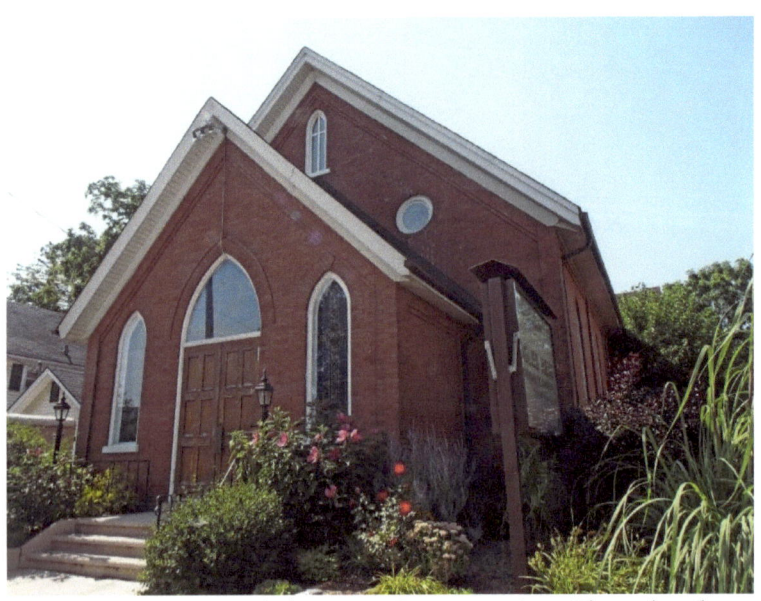

92 Main Street – Eagle's Nest Community Church – lancet windows, transom window above door, rose window

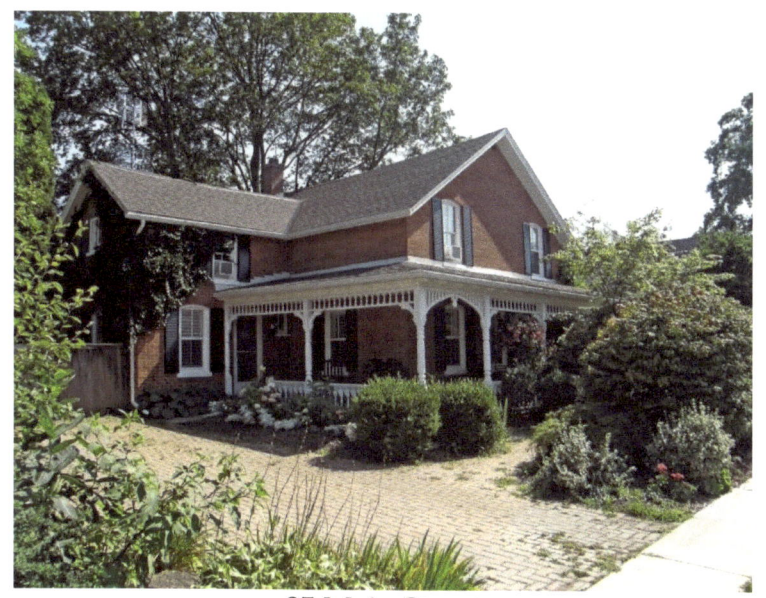

95 Main Street

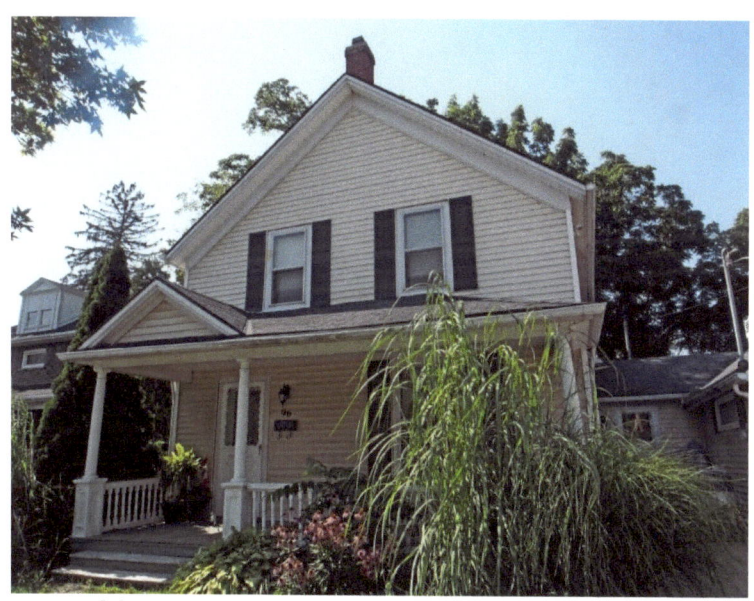

96 Main Street – pediment above entrance

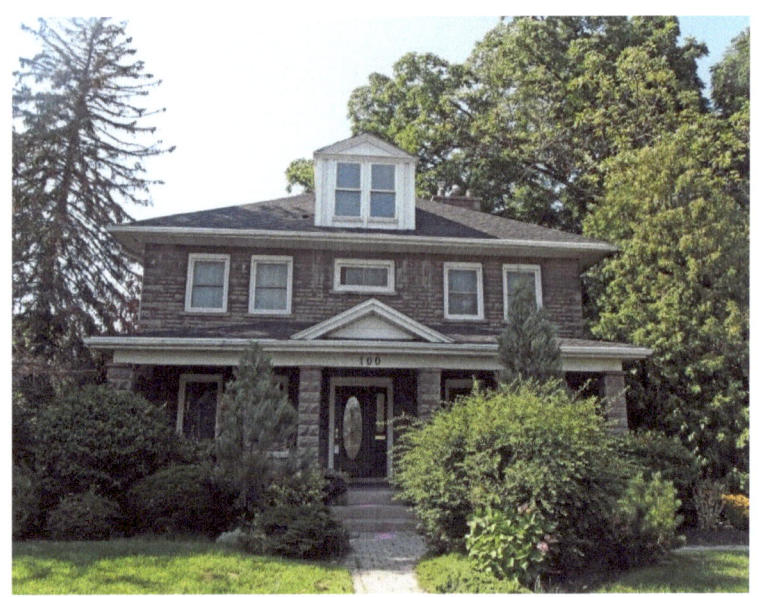

100 Main Street - dormer

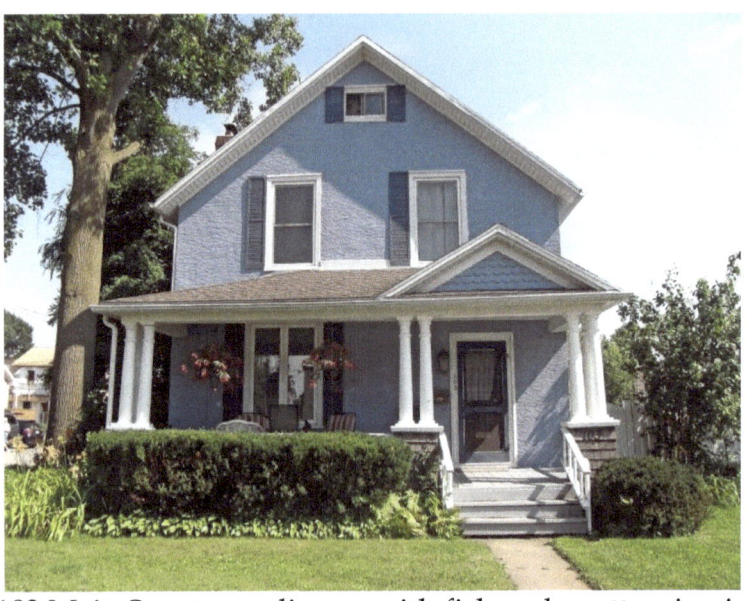

103 Main Street – pediment with fish scale patterning in tympanum

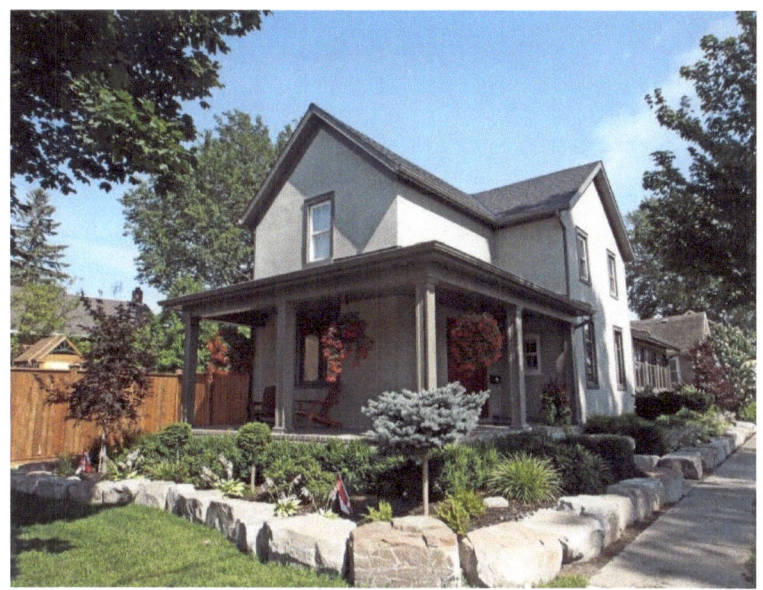

Main Street

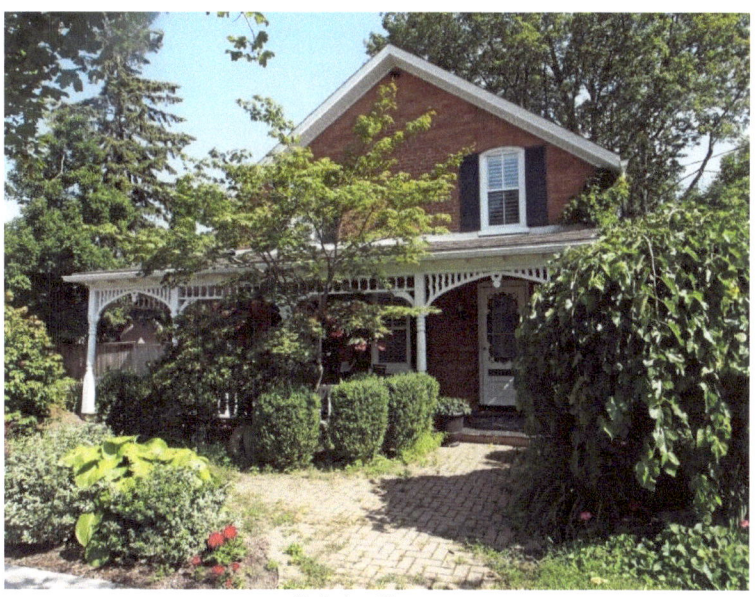

Main Street

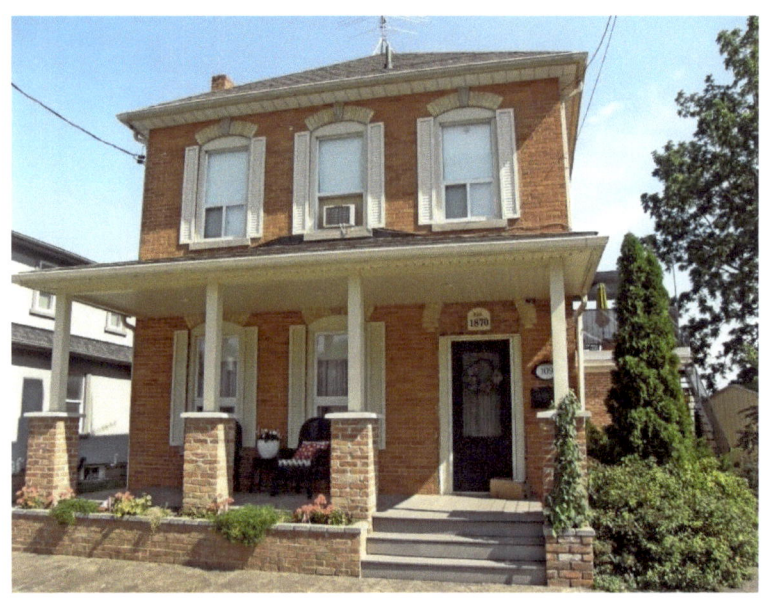

109 Main Street – two storey, Italianate, hipped roof, keystones and voussoirs above windows and door

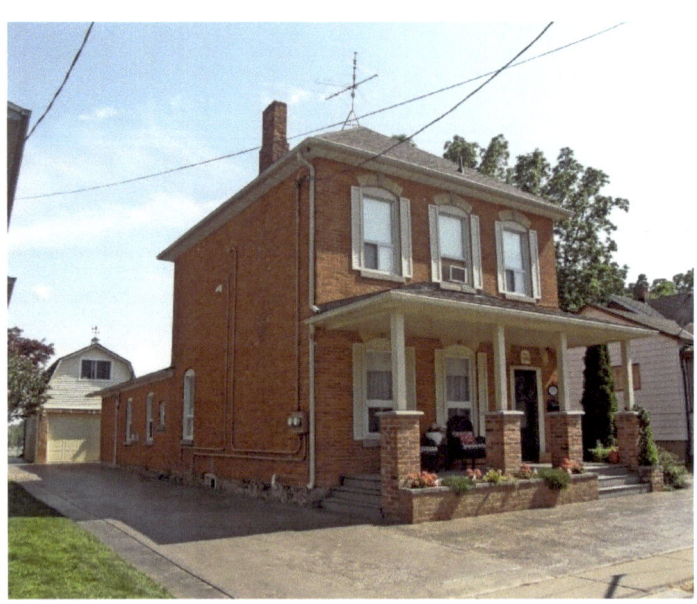

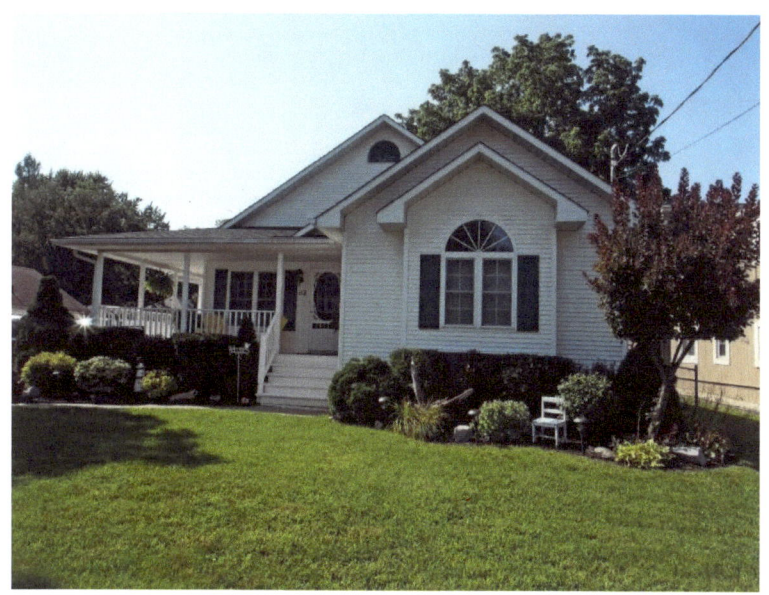

112 Main Street - Vernacular

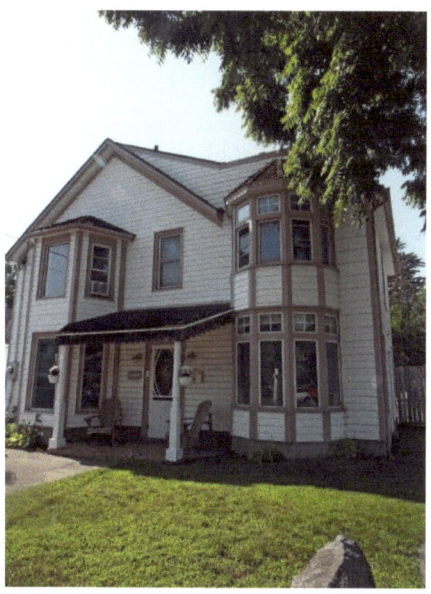

118 Main Street – two-storey bay windows

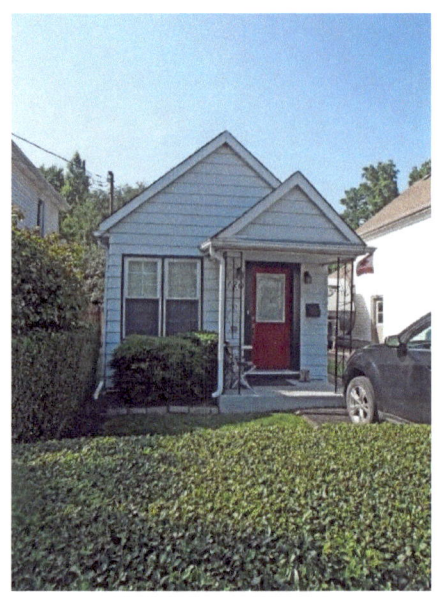

120 Main Street

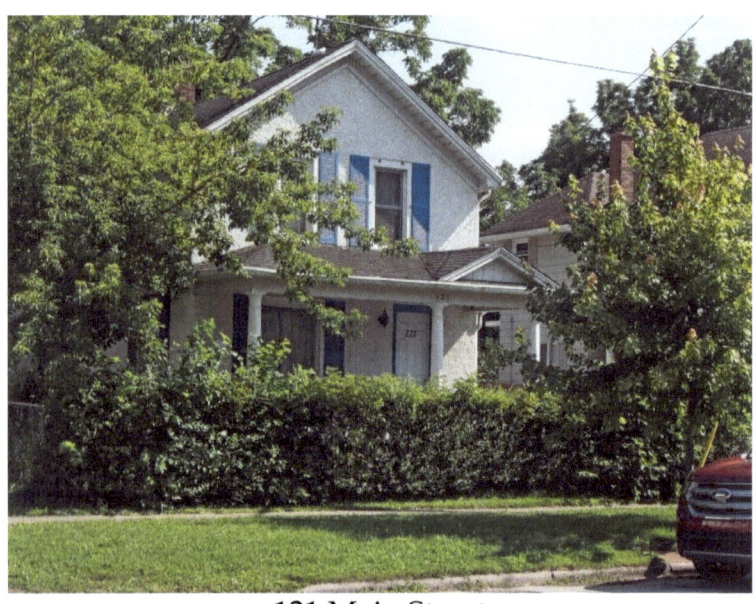

121 Main Street

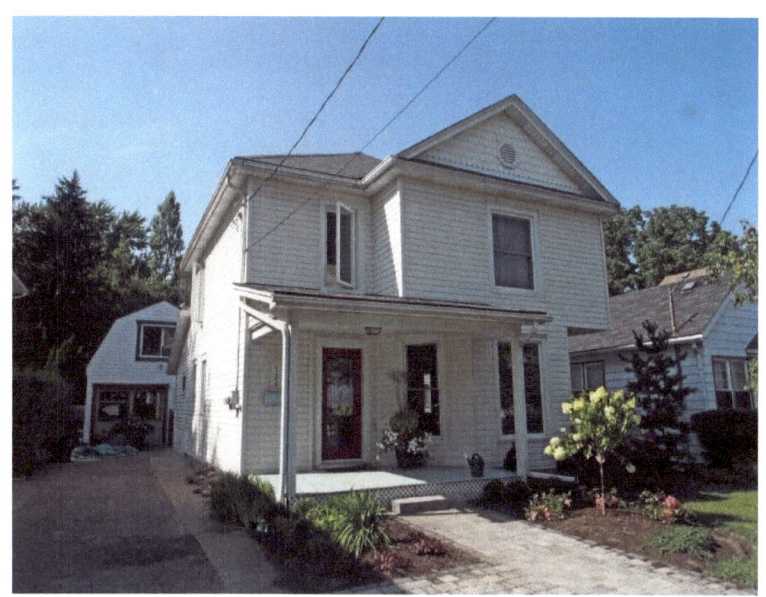

122 Main Street

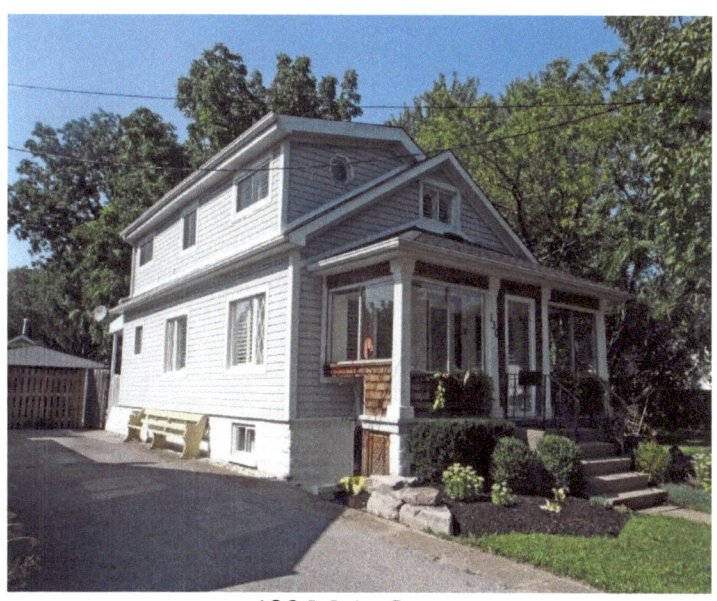

130 Main Street

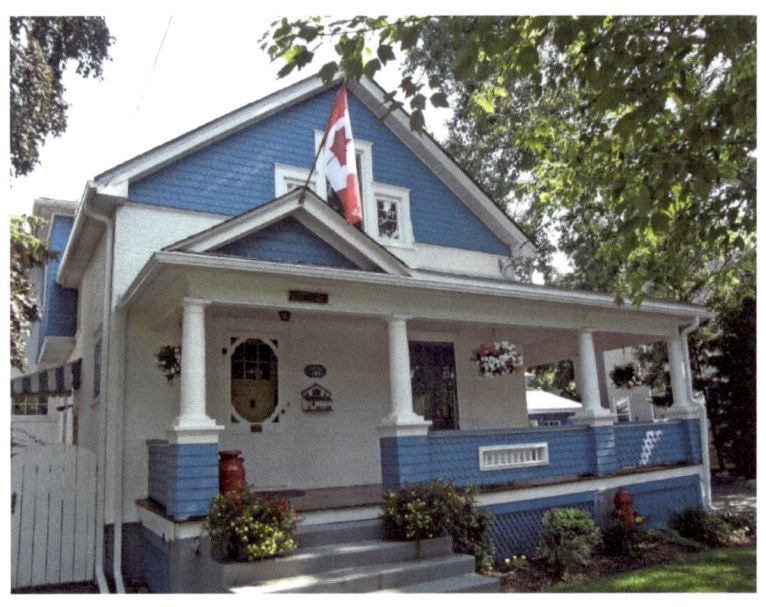

127 Main Street – pediment, Palladian window in gable

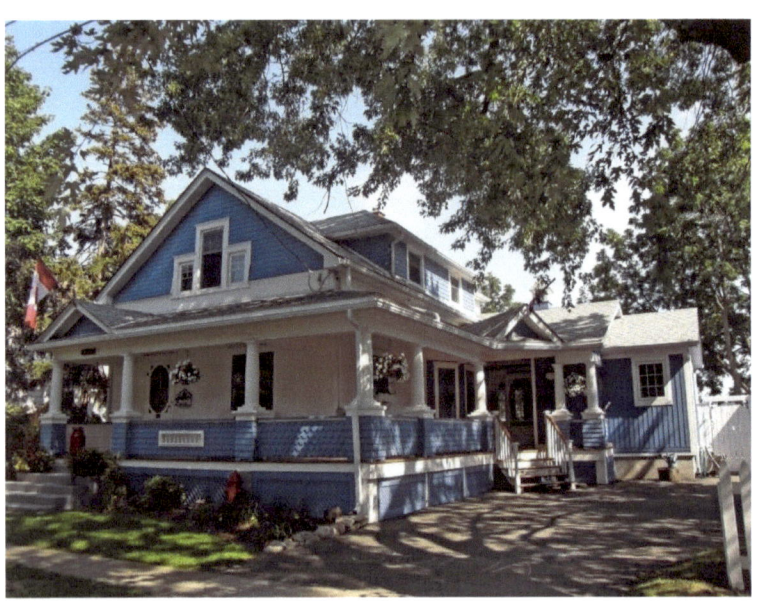

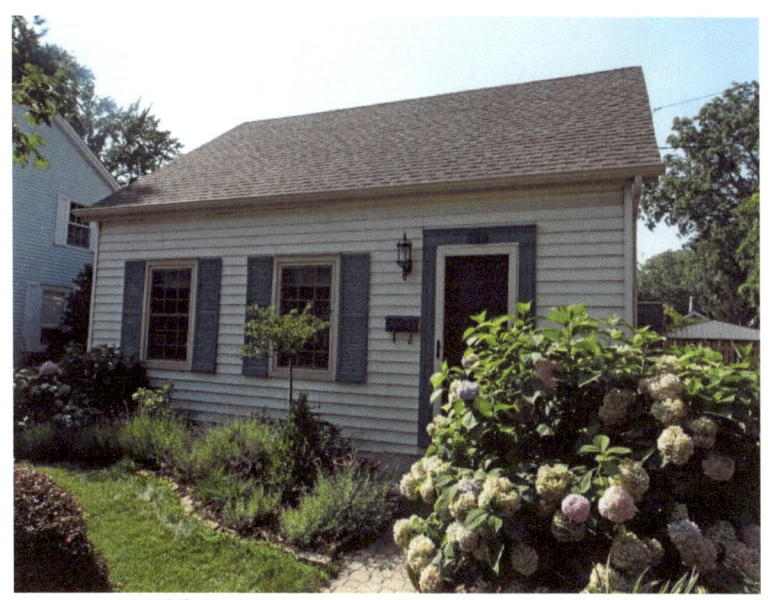

132 Main Street – Regency Cottage

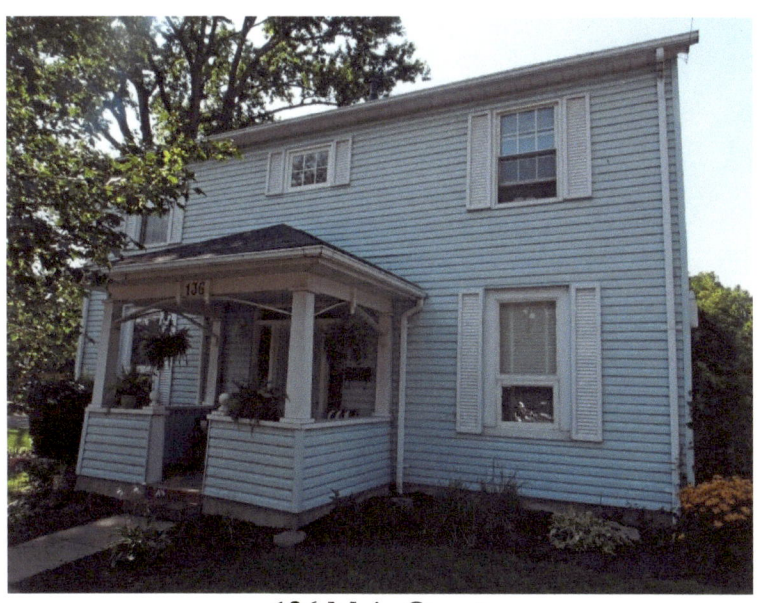

136 Main Street

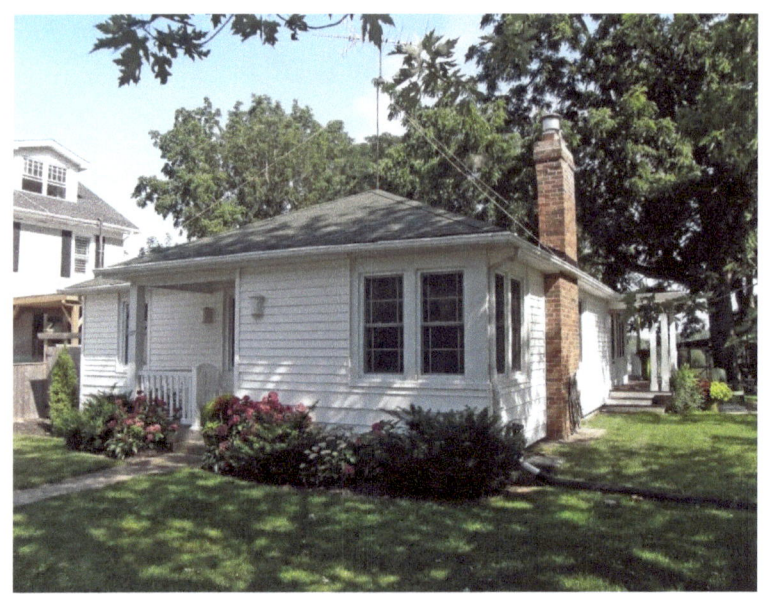

137 Main Street – Regency Cottage

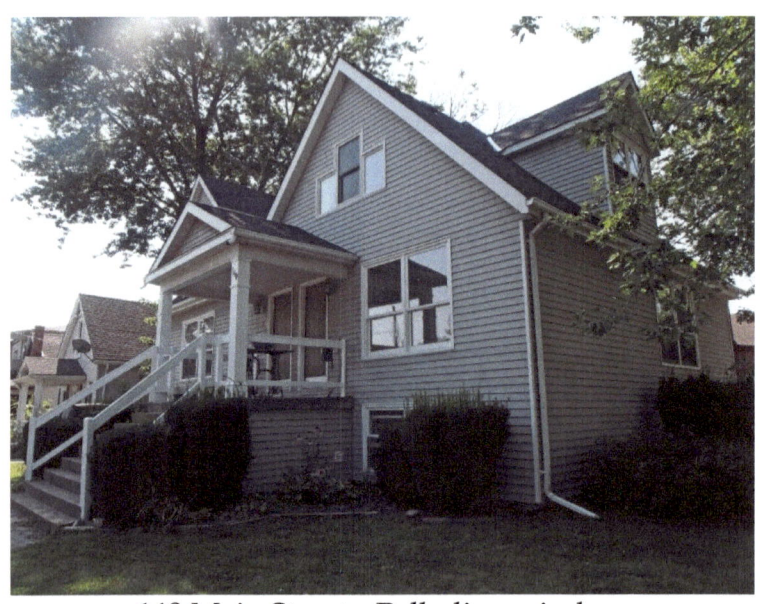

140 Main Street - Palladian window

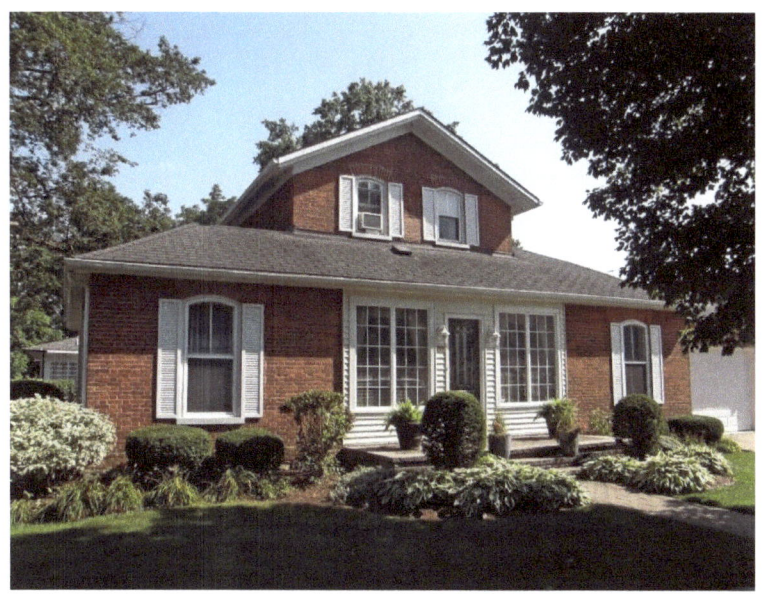

141 Main Street – large dormer in Regency Cottage

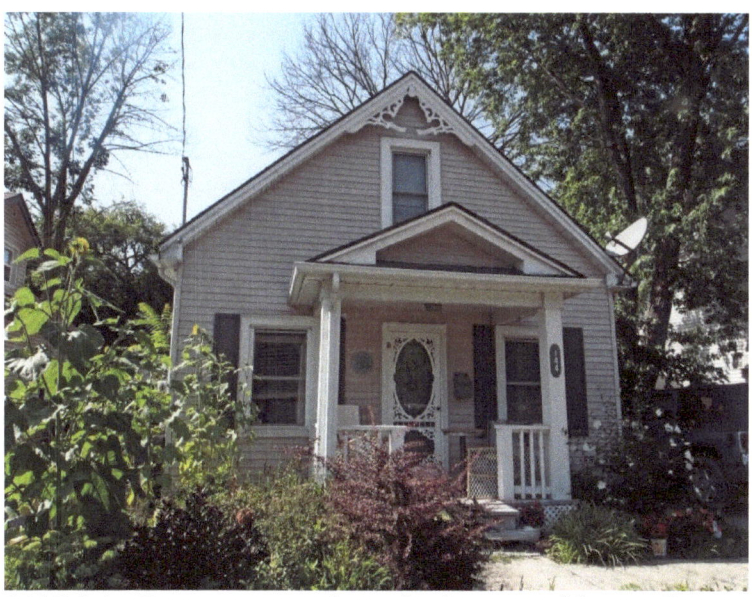

144 Main Street – verge board trim on gable, pediment

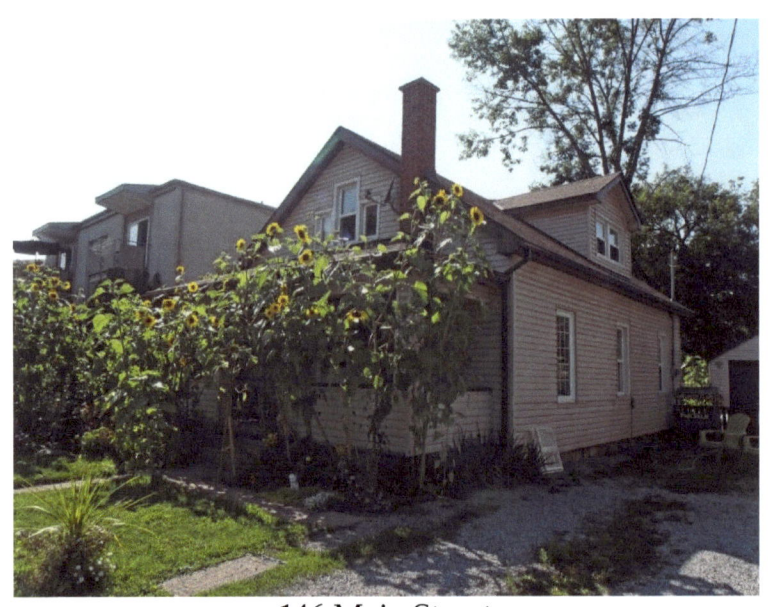

146 Main Street

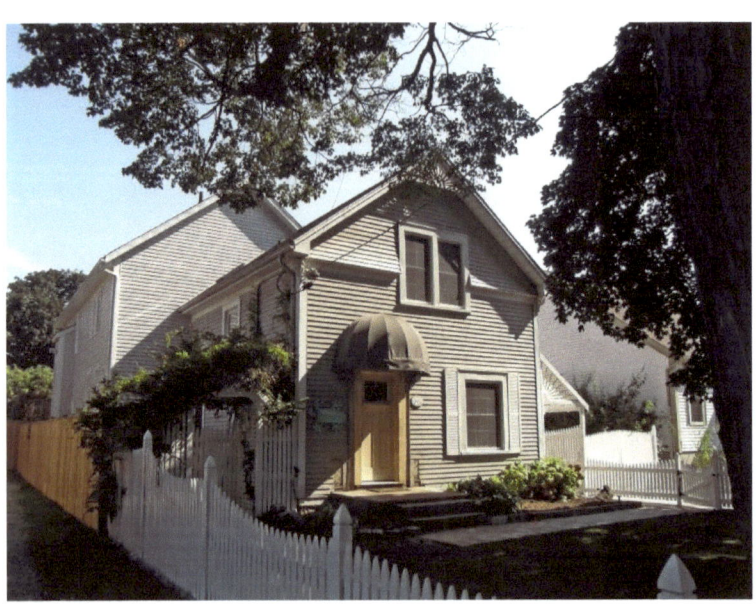

149 Main Street

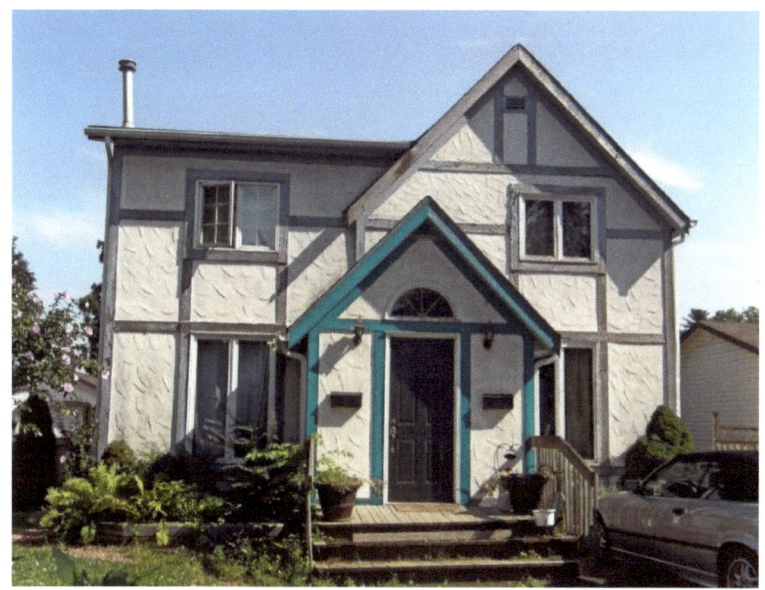

Main Street – Tudor timbering on stucco

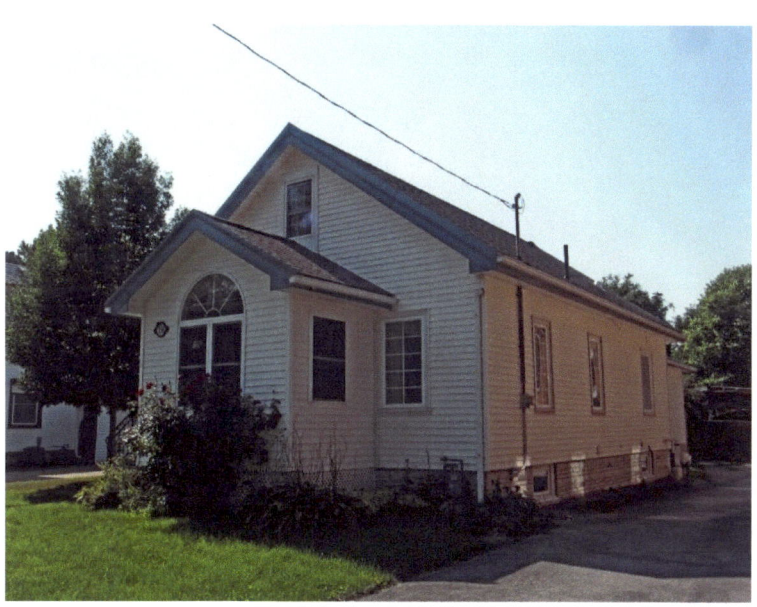

158 Main Street

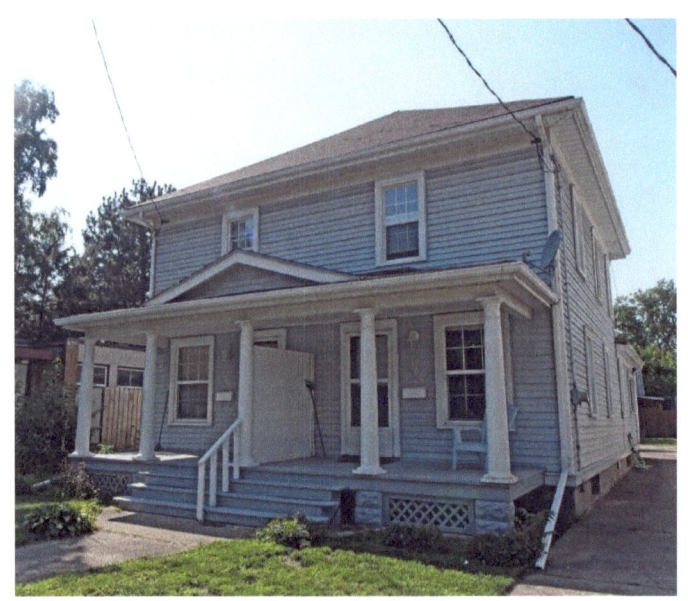

164 Main Street - pediment

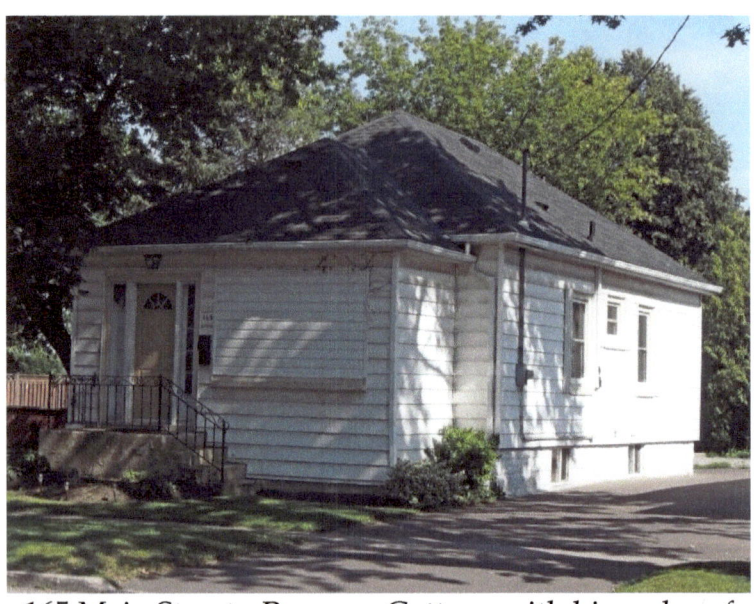

165 Main Street - Regency Cottage with hipped roof

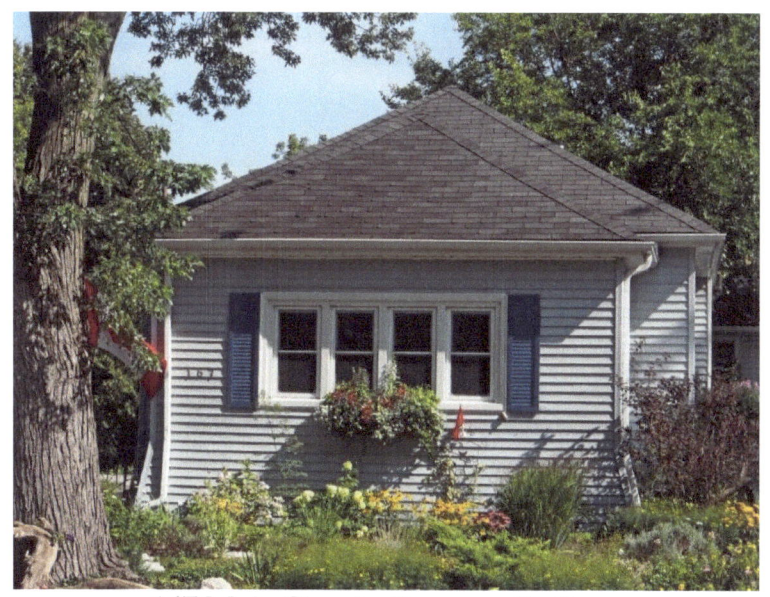
167 Main Street - Regency Cottage

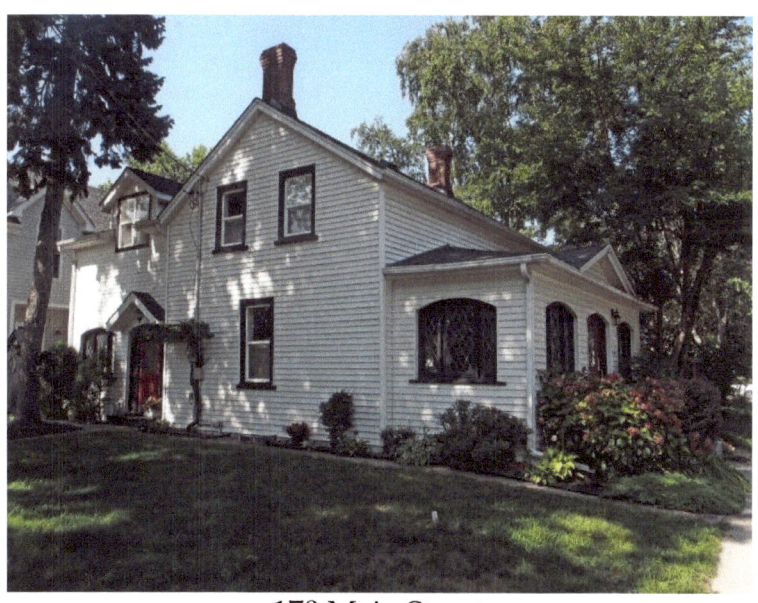
170 Main Street

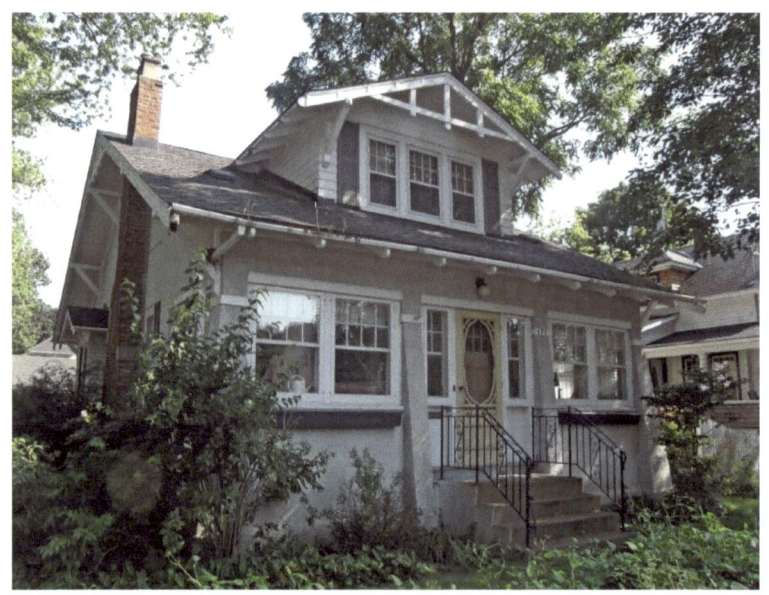

171 Main Street - dormer

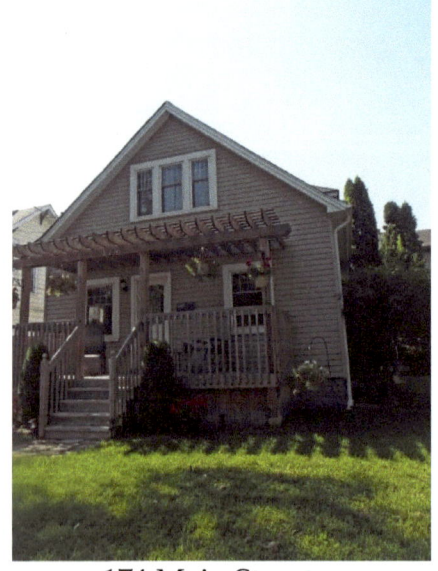

174 Main Street

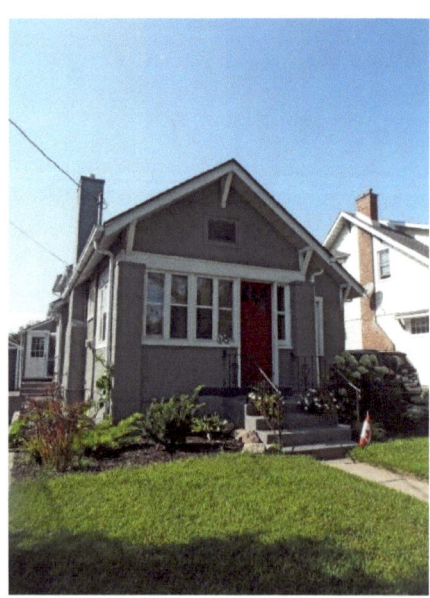

178 Main Street

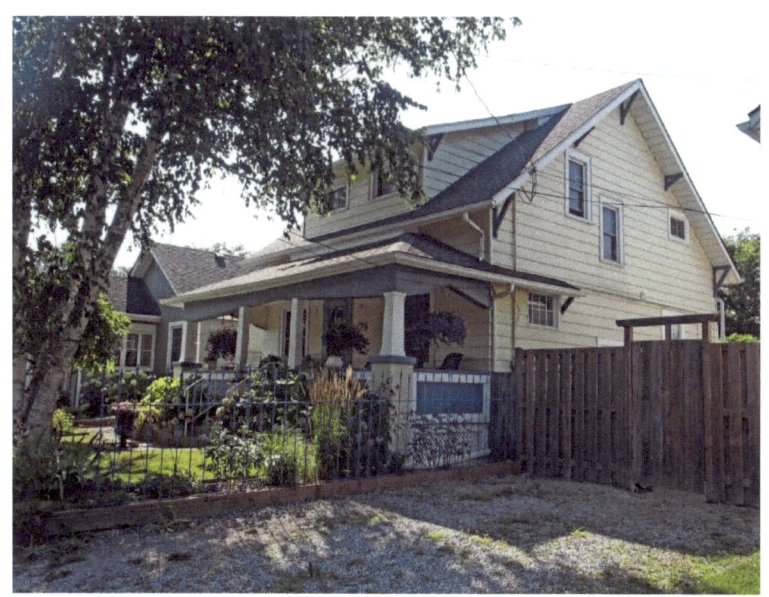

176 Main Street – shed dormer

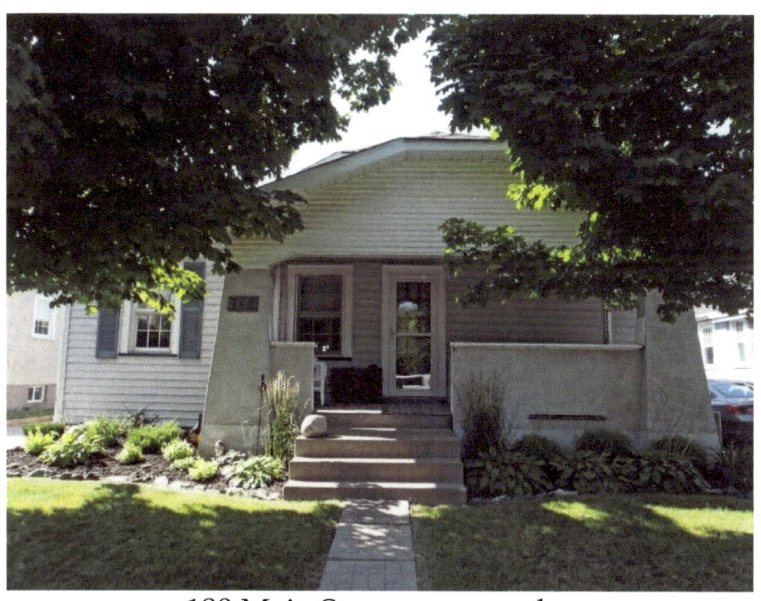

180 Main Street - vernacular

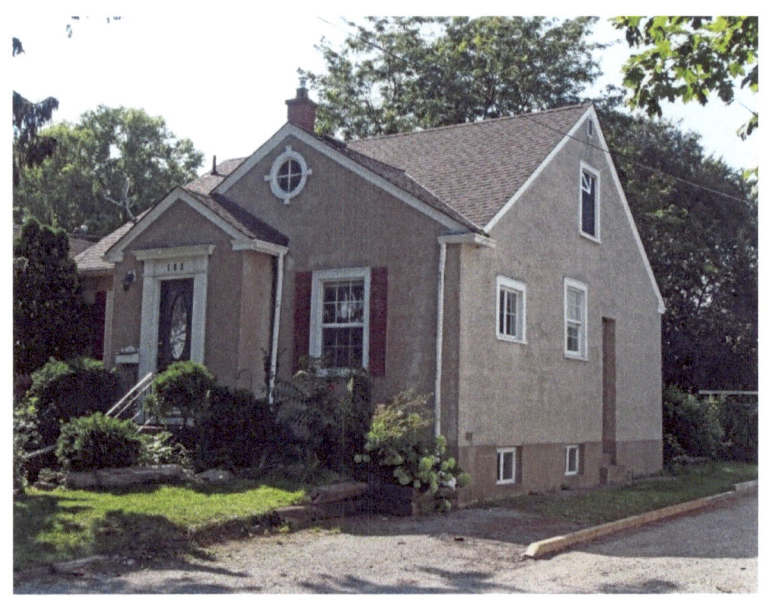

182 Main Street

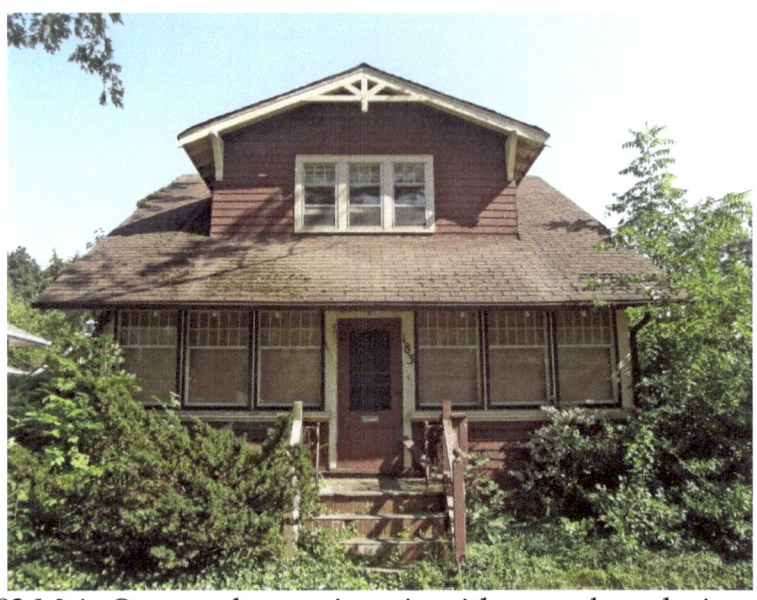

183 Main Street – dormer in attic with verge board trim on gable

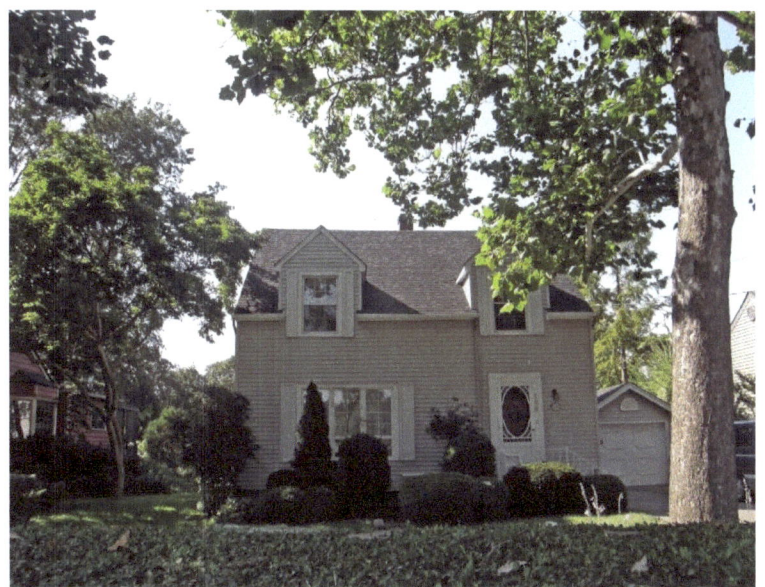

196 Main Street - dormers

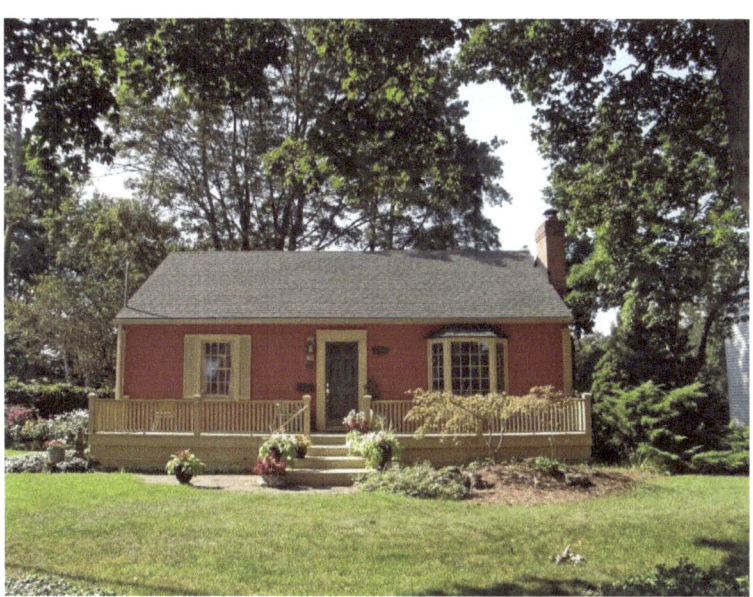

200 Main Street - Regency Cottage

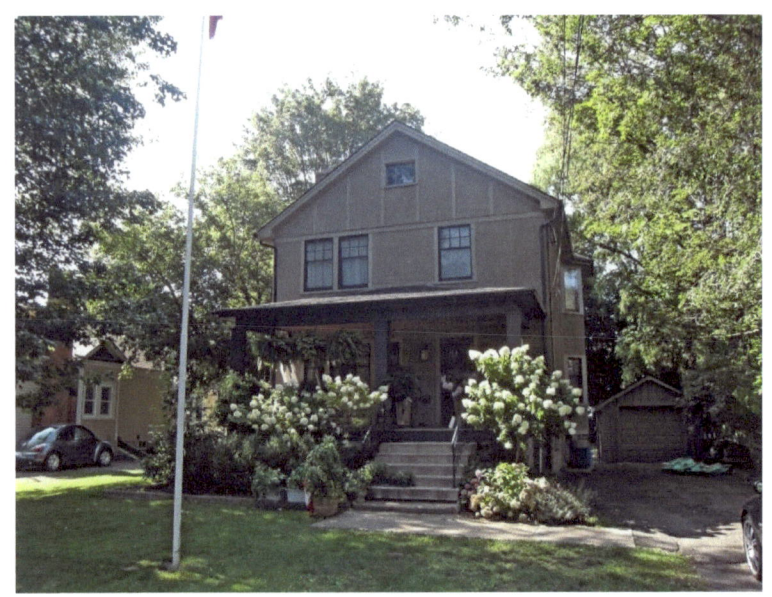

Main Street

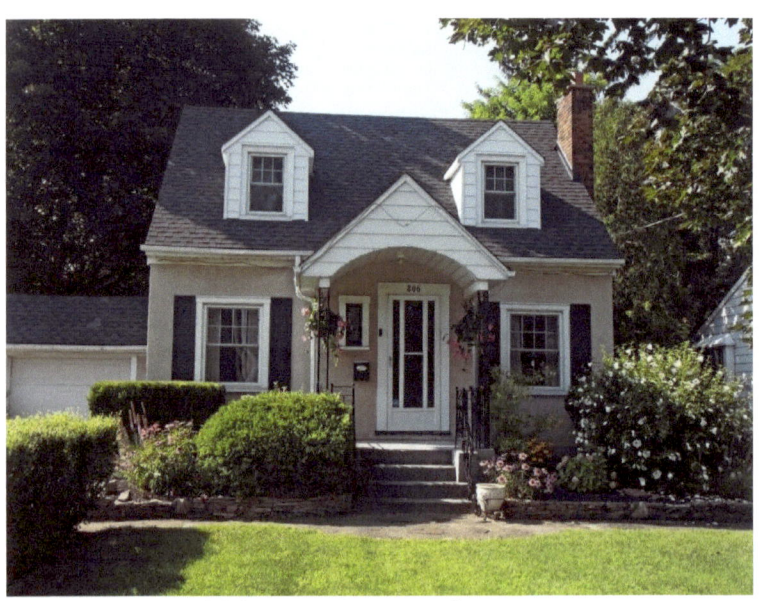

206 Main Street - dormers

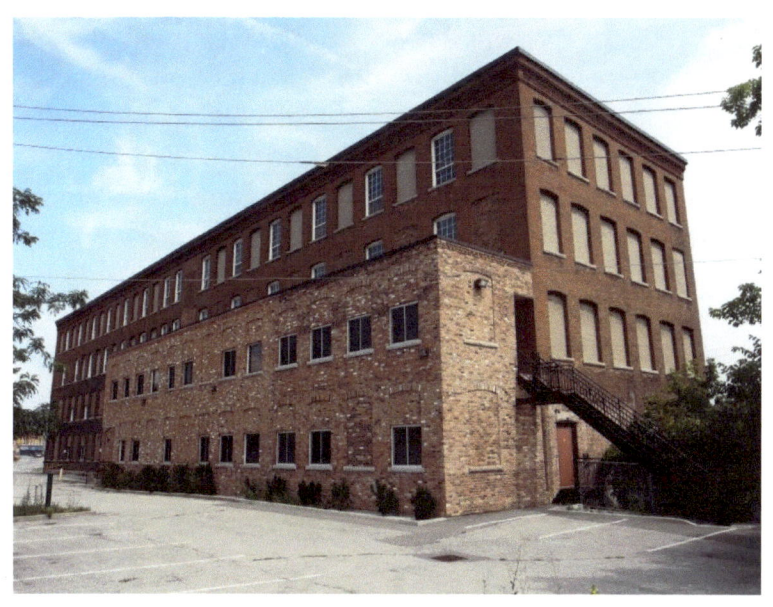

63 Lakeport Road

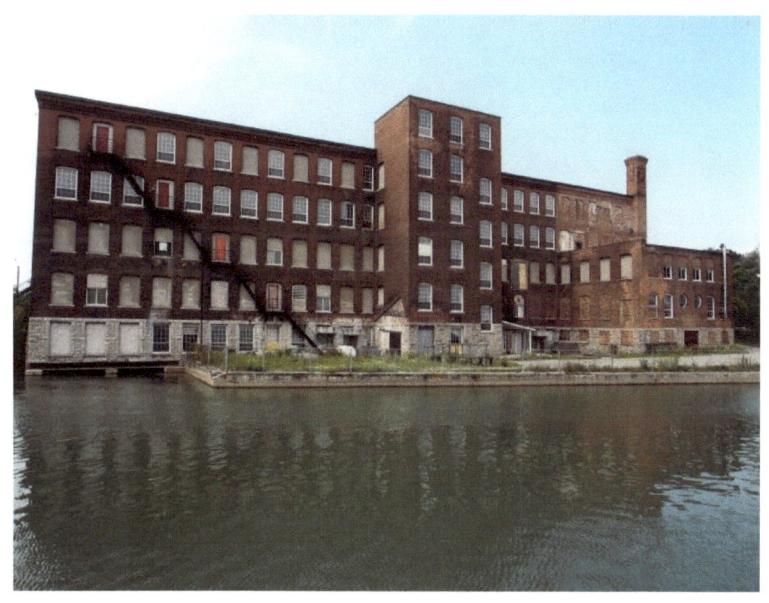

    The factory at 63 Lakeport Road was built between 1899 and 1900 for the Maple Leaf Rubber Company. In 1955 A. Stewart Howes established Lincoln Fabrics Limited as a weaver of specialty fabrics. Stewart's son David assumed leadership of the company from 1983 until his death in 2015. Both father and son were committed to a family oriented business employing a loyal and skilled workforce from the local community. Both were involved in the community

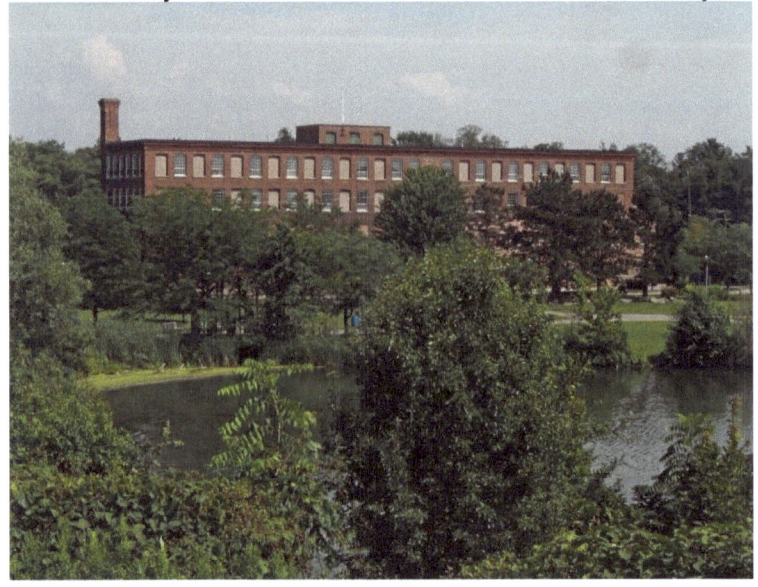

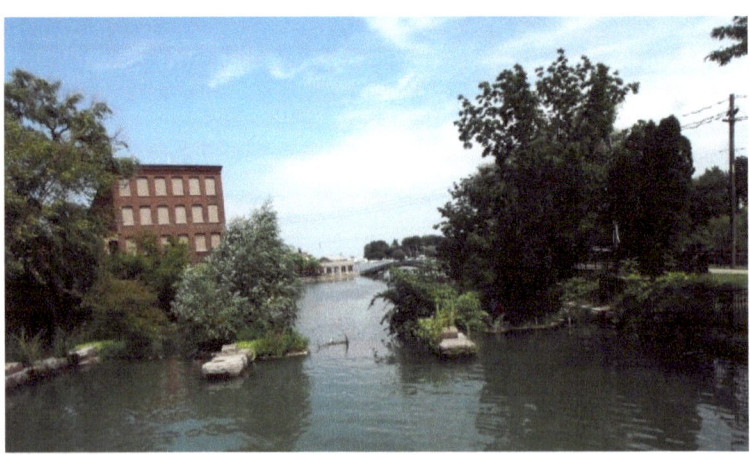

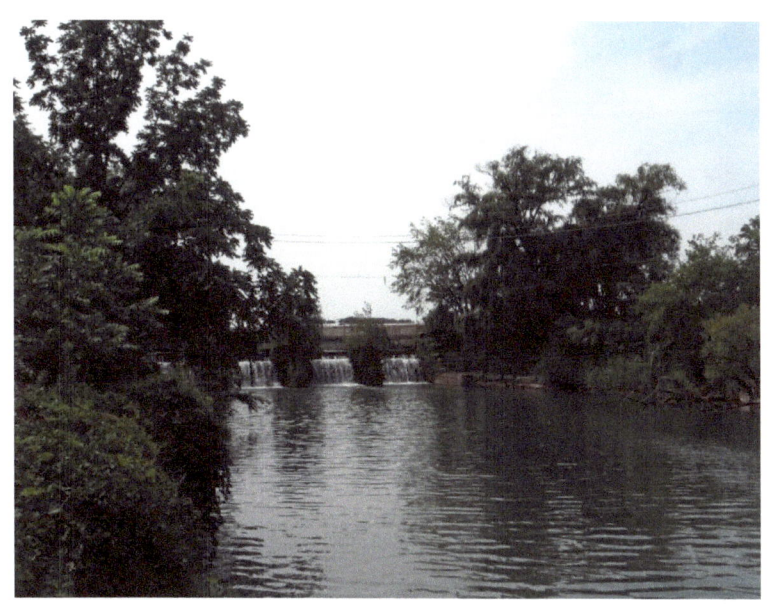

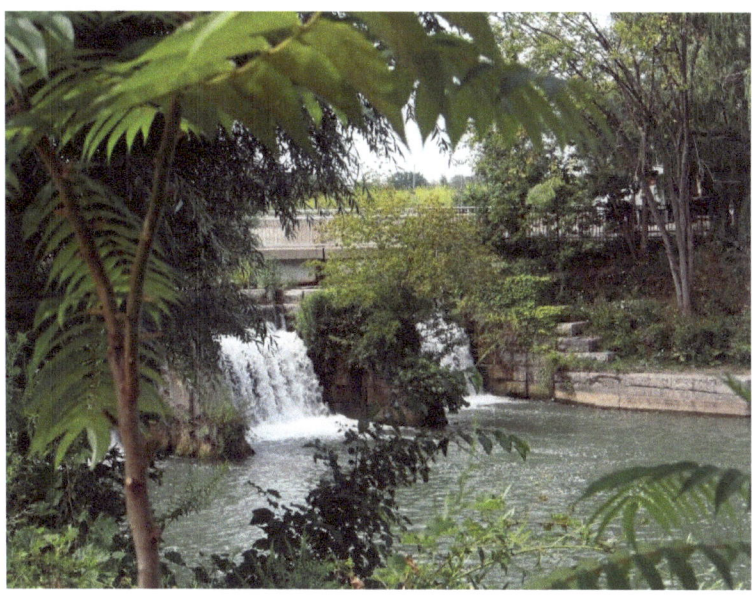

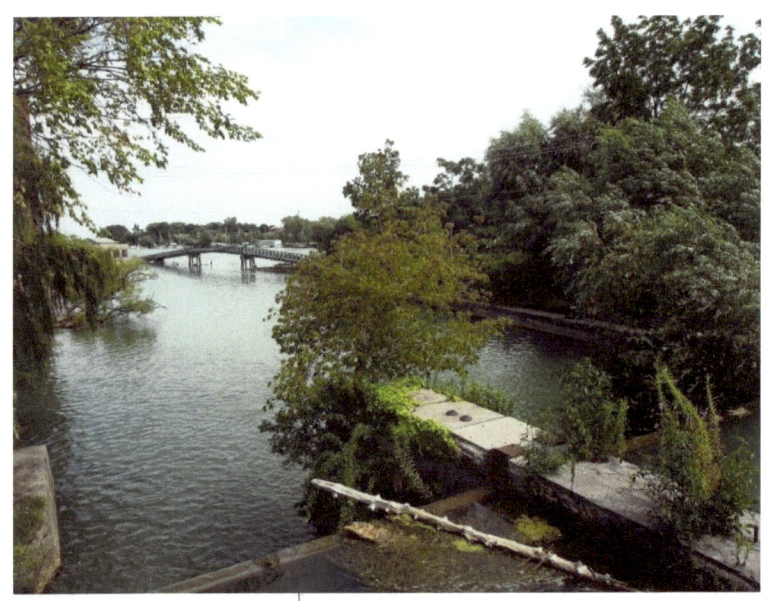

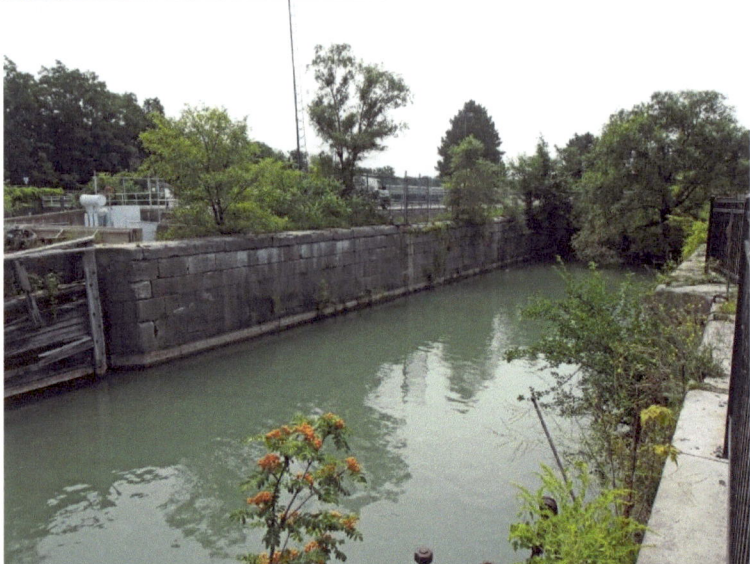

This stone lock was the Welland Canal's northern terminus from 1882 to 1930 and played a central role in the life of the village of Port Dalhousie. This lock was part of the Third Welland Canal. The lock was 270 feet long, 45 feet wide and 12 feet deep.

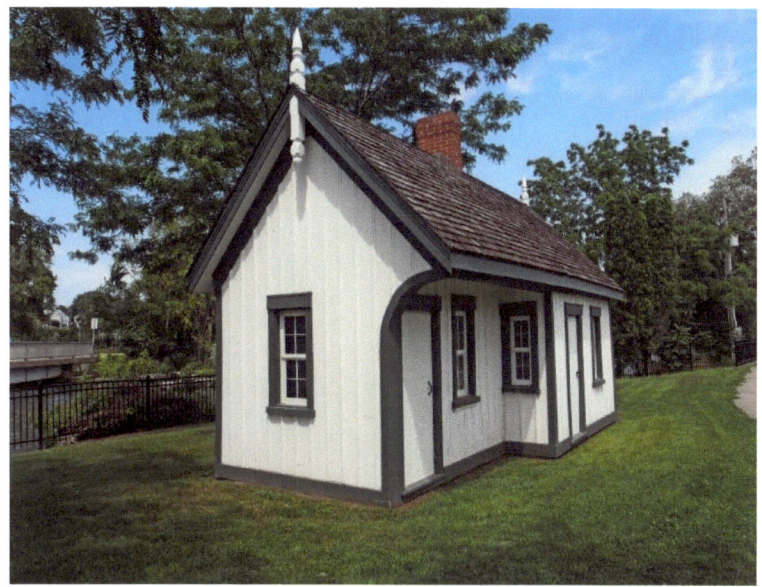

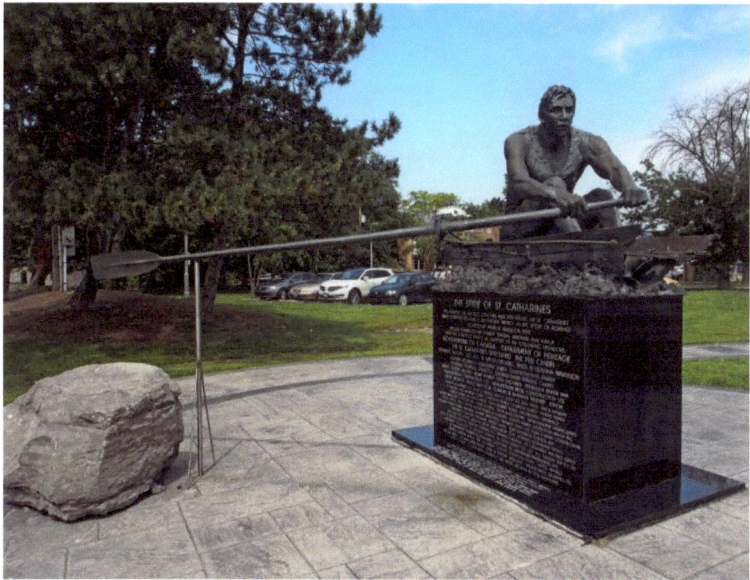

The Spirit of St. Catharines was sculpted by Perry P. Wakulich in 1999 to honour the athletes, coaches and volunteers who continue to have a significant impact on the sport of rowing.

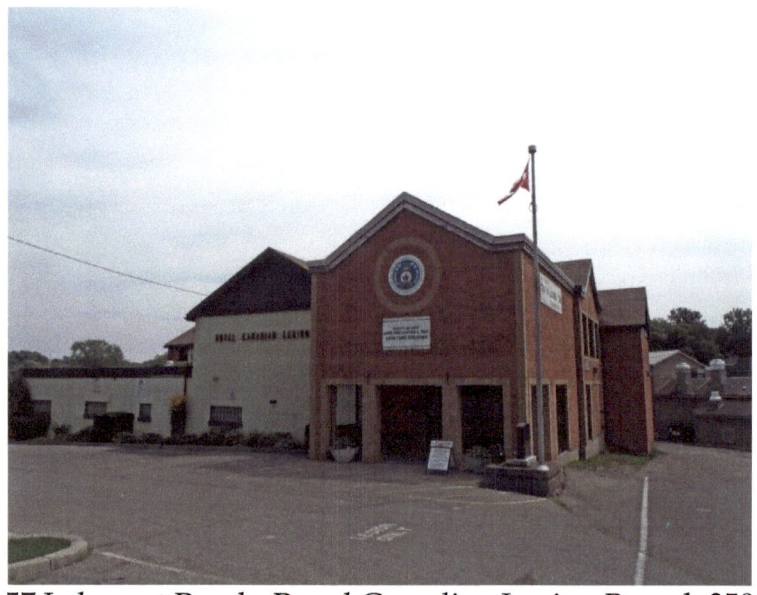
57 Lakeport Road - Royal Canadian Legion Branch 350

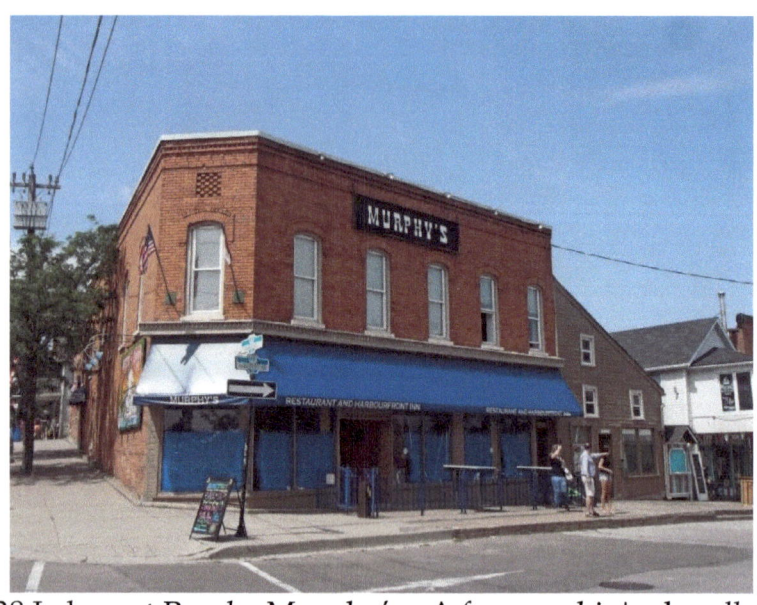
38 Lakeport Road – Murphy's - A former ship's chandler building has been converted into a trendy harbor side restaurant.

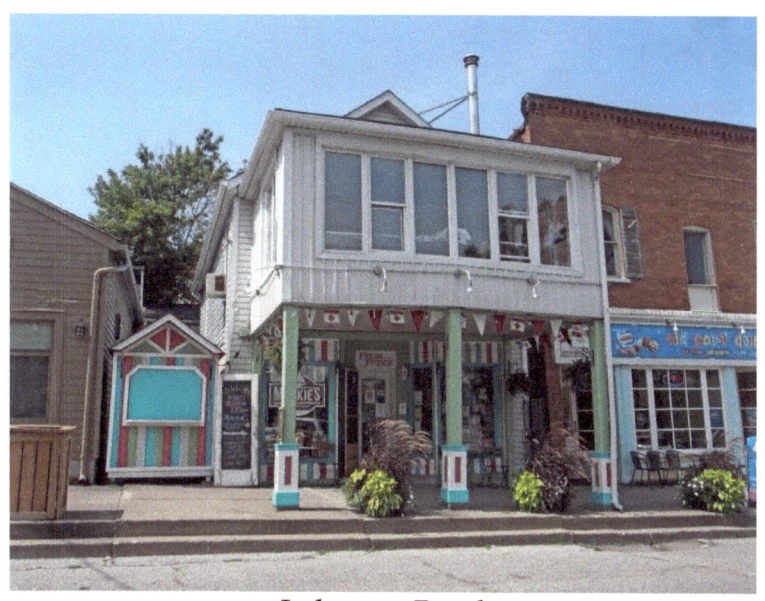

Lakeport Road

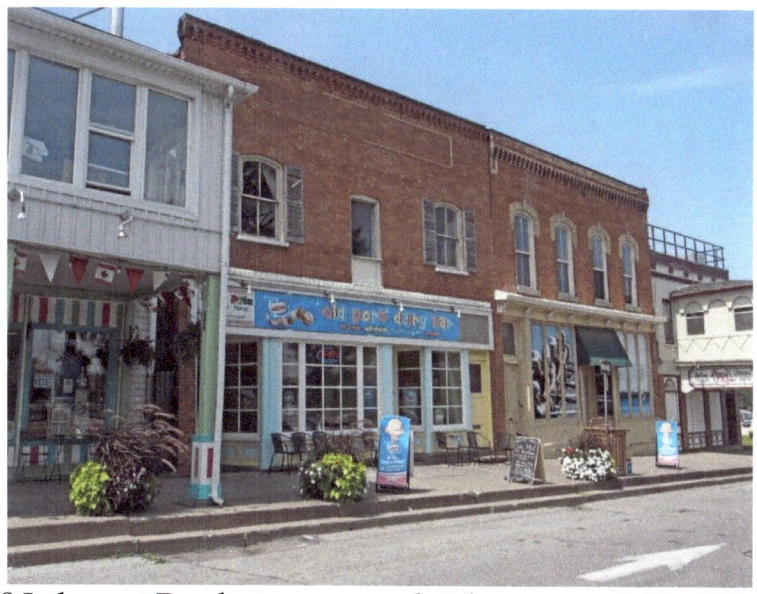

18 Lakeport Road – two-storey brick commercial building

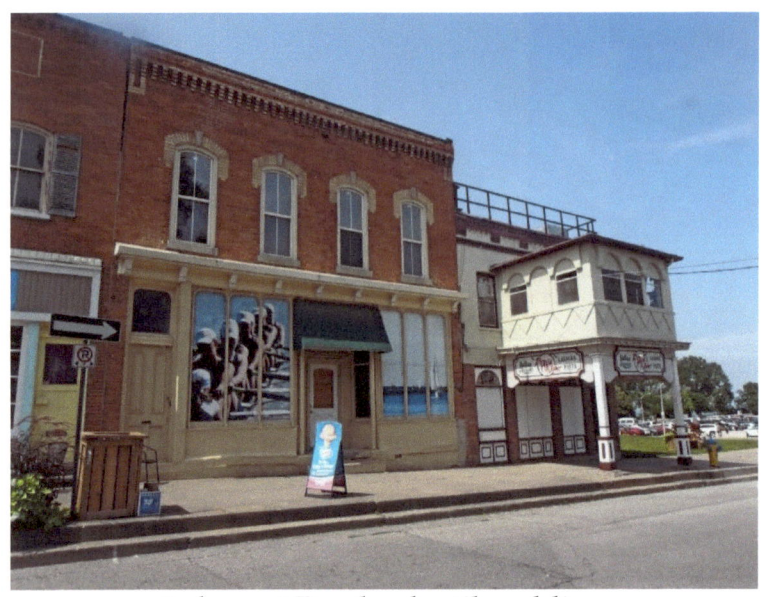
Lakeport Road – dentil molding

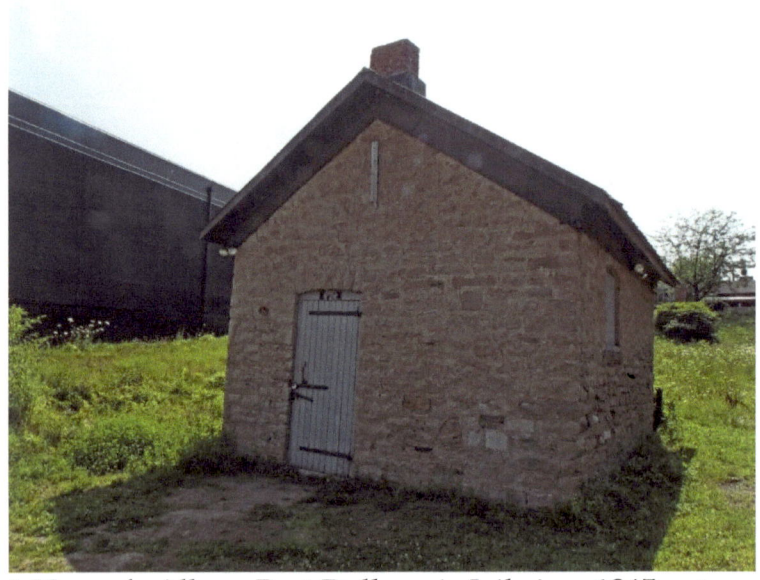
1 Hogan's Alley - Port Dalhousie Jail circa 1845 - stone

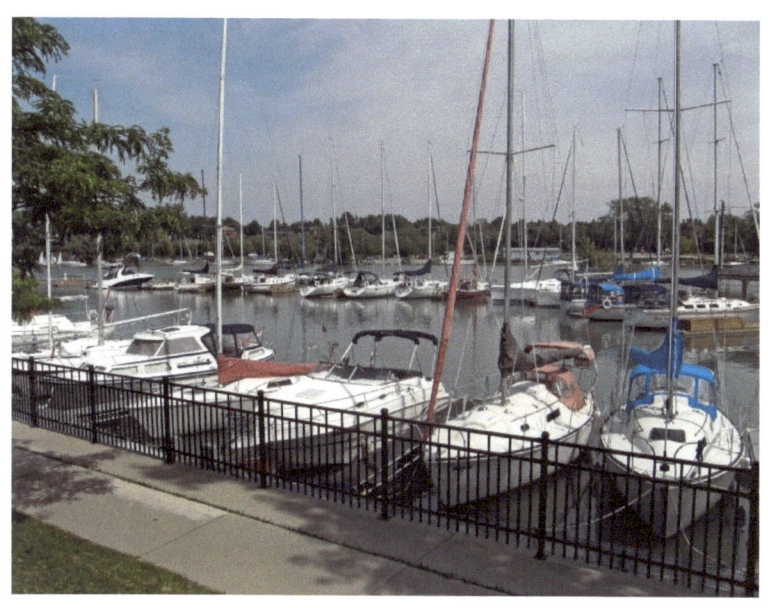

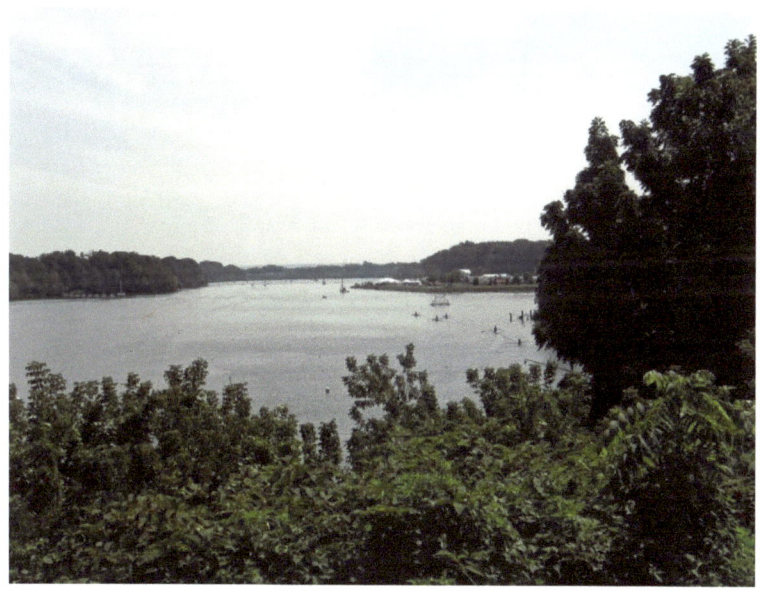

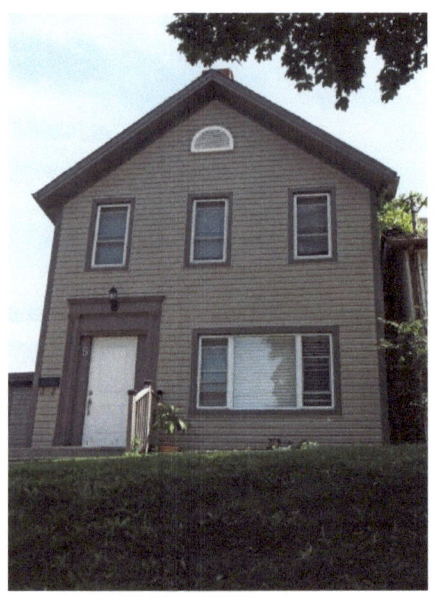

5 Canal Street

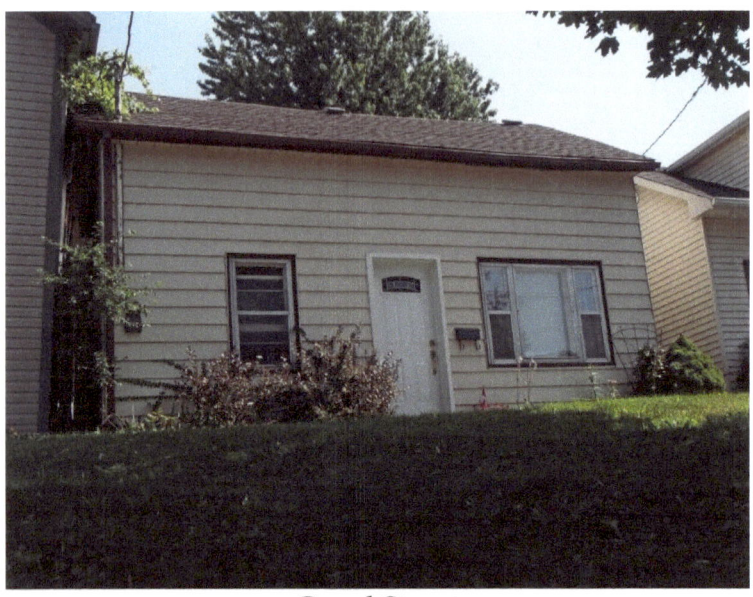

Canal Street

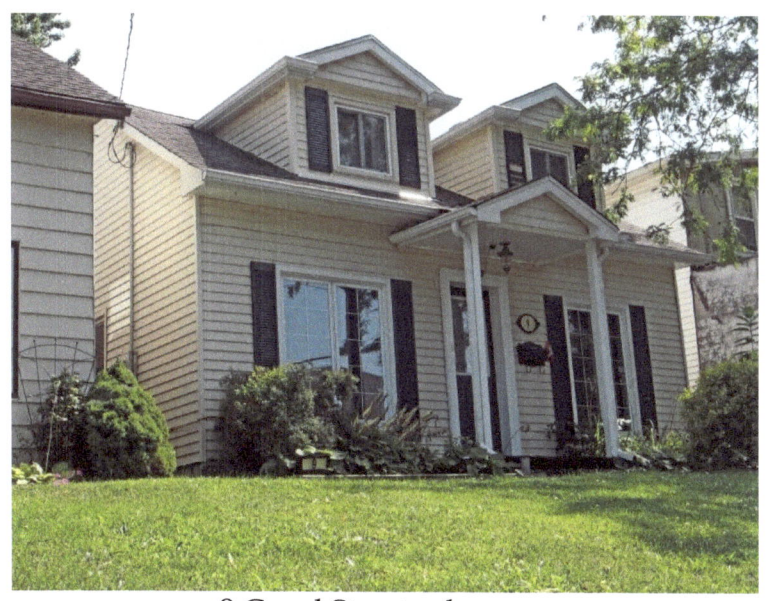

9 Canal Street - dormers

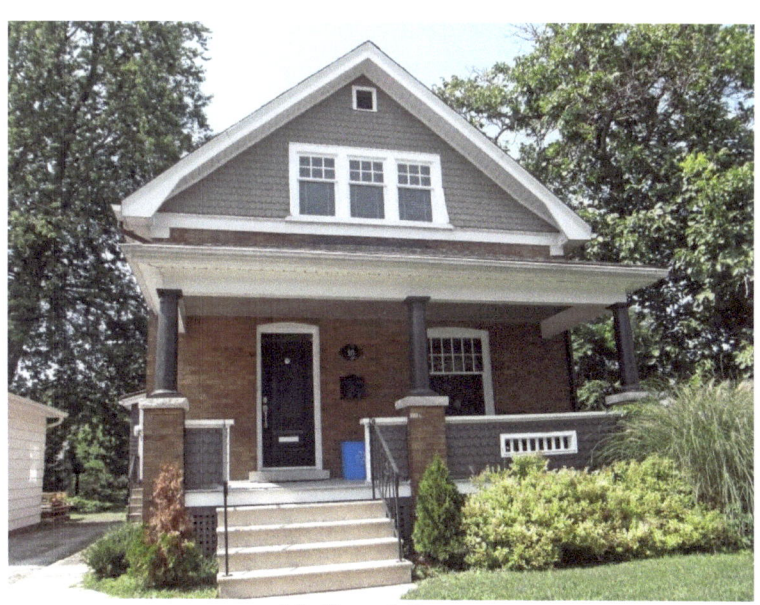

10 Canal Street

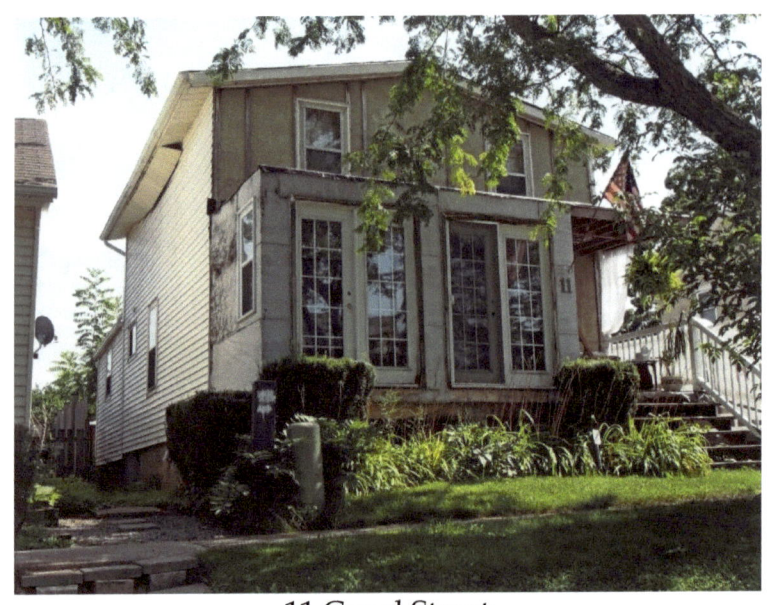

11 Canal Street

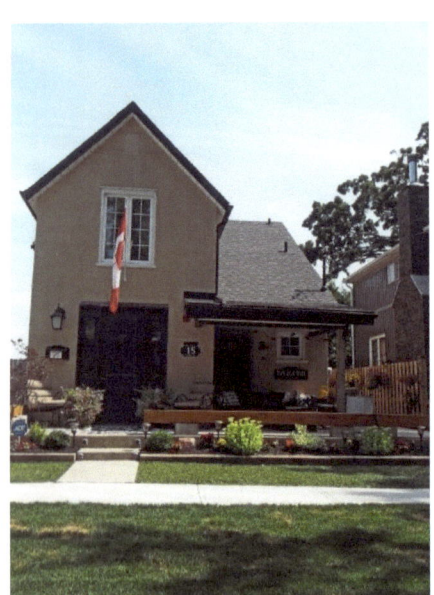

15 Canal Street

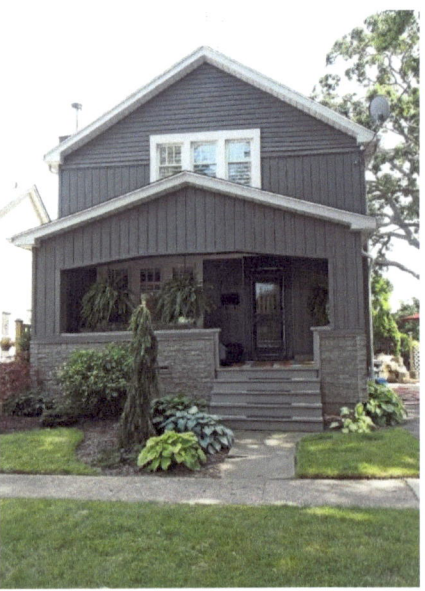

Canal Street

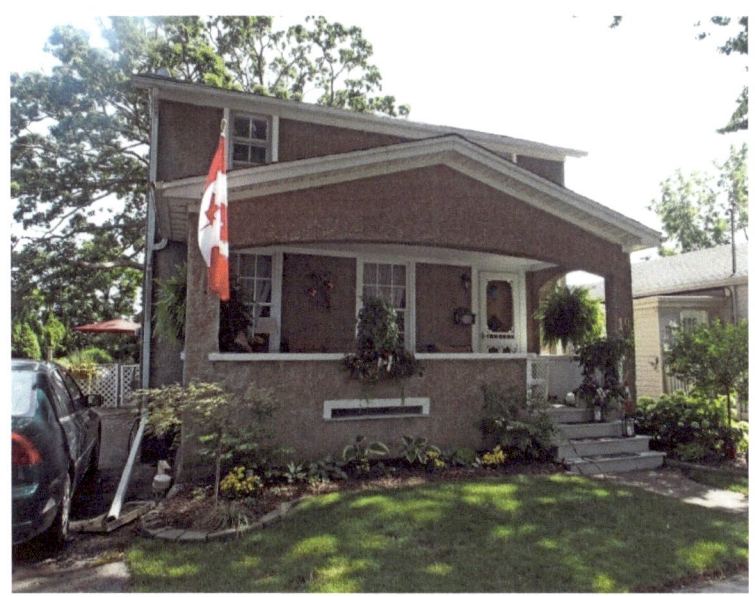

19 Canal Street

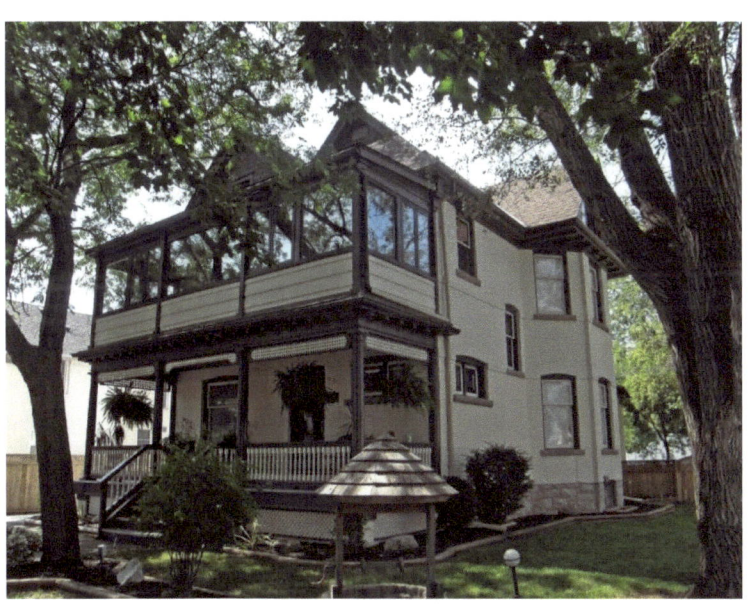

20 Canal Street

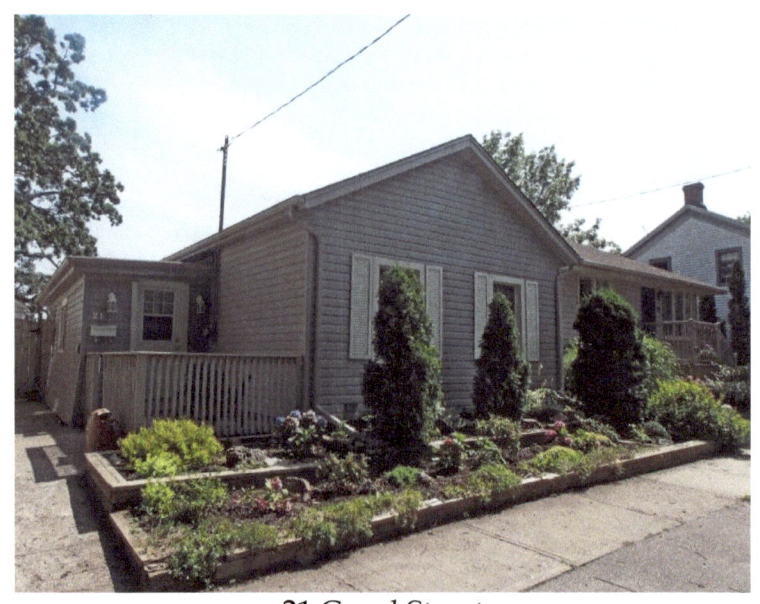

21 Canal Street

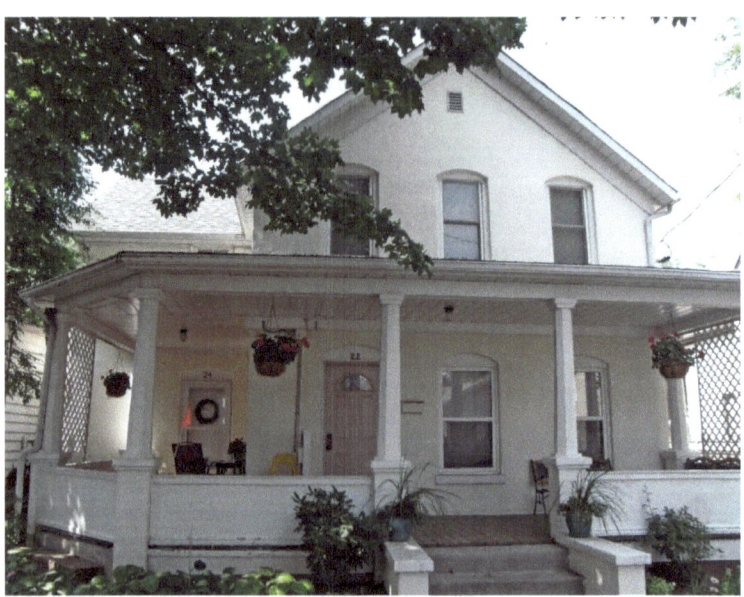

22 Canal Street

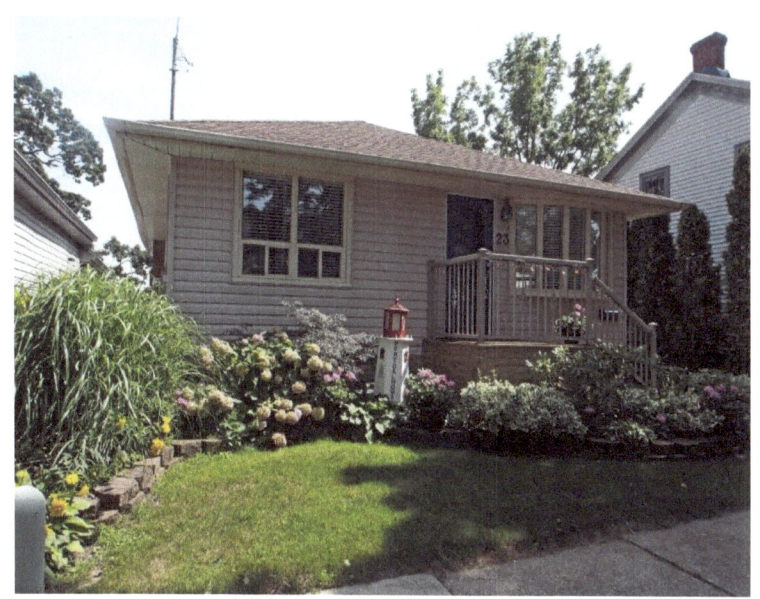

23 Canal Street - Regency Cottage

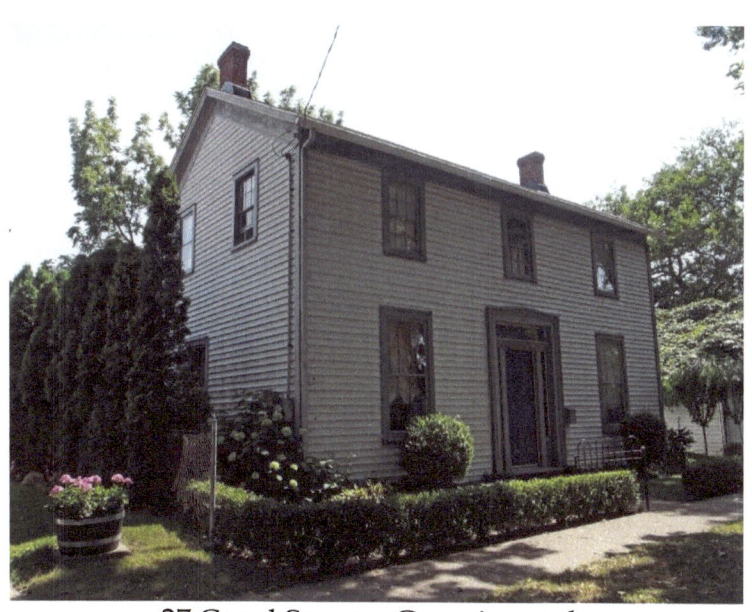

27 Canal Street – Georgian style

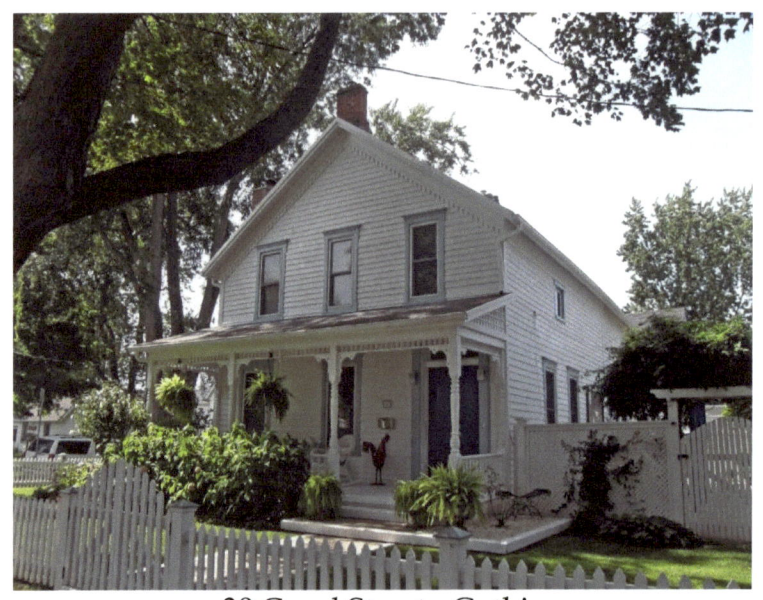

30 Canal Street - Gothic

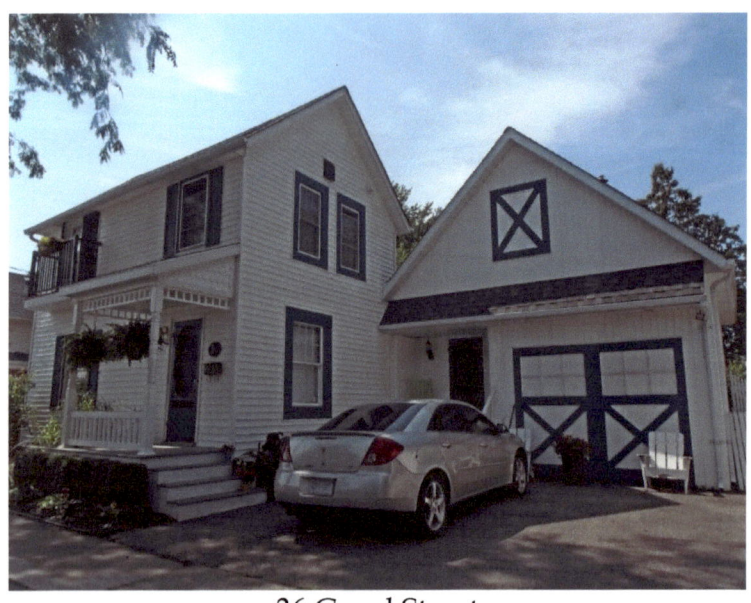

36 Canal Street

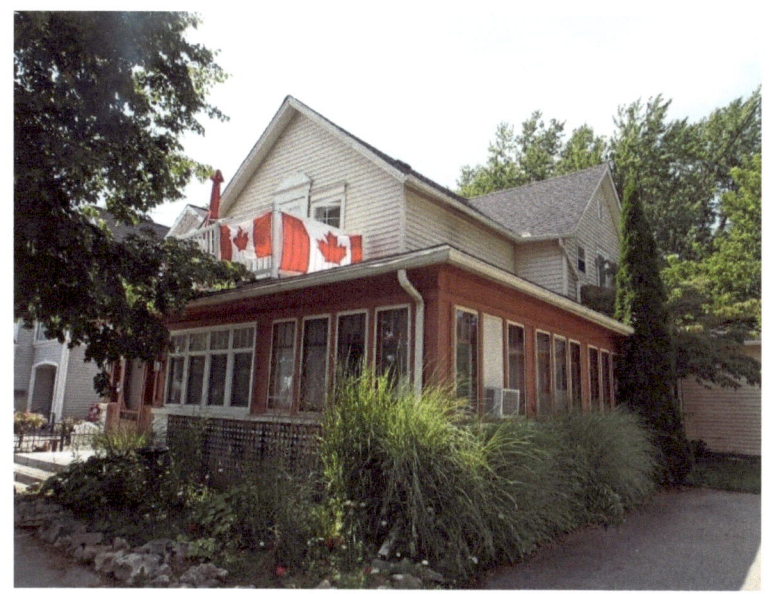

40 Canal Street

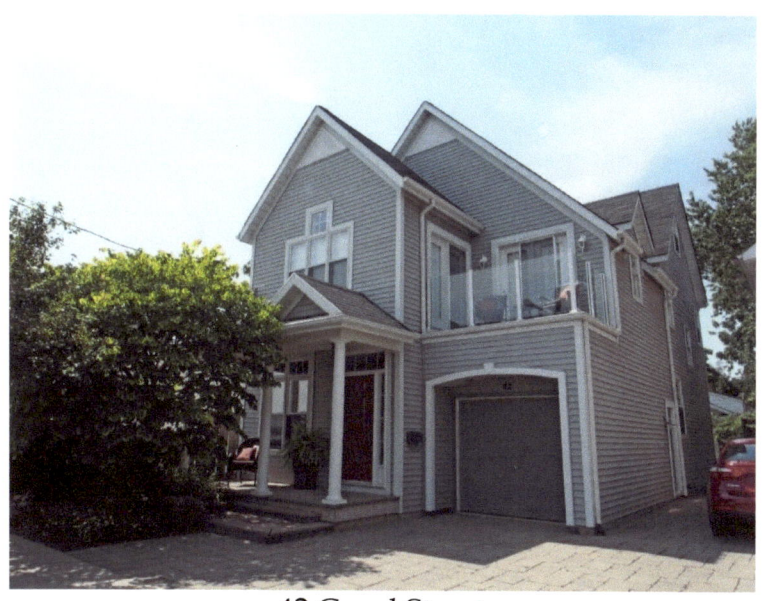

42 Canal Street

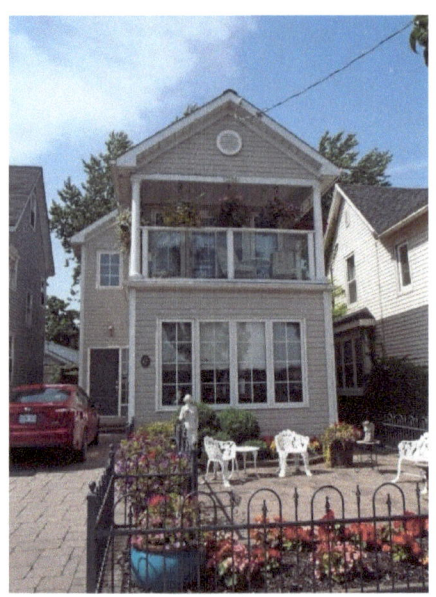

42½ Canal Street

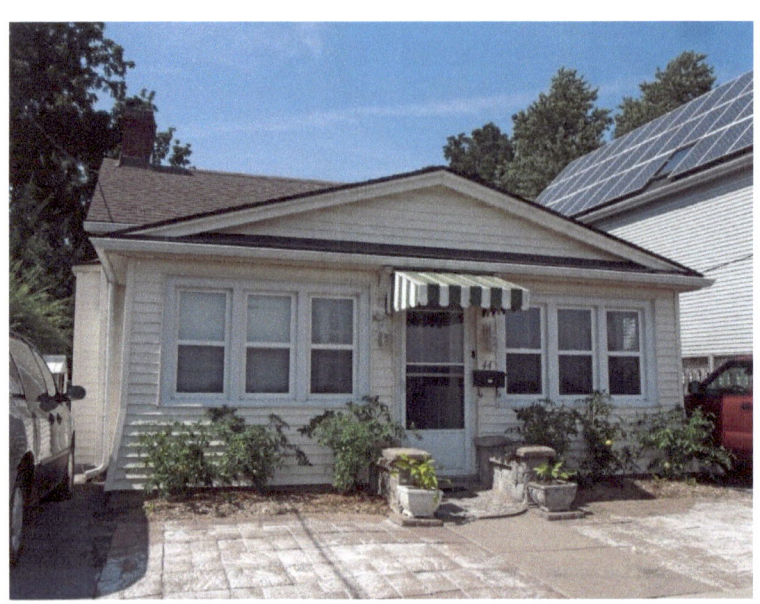

44 Canal Street - Regency Cottage

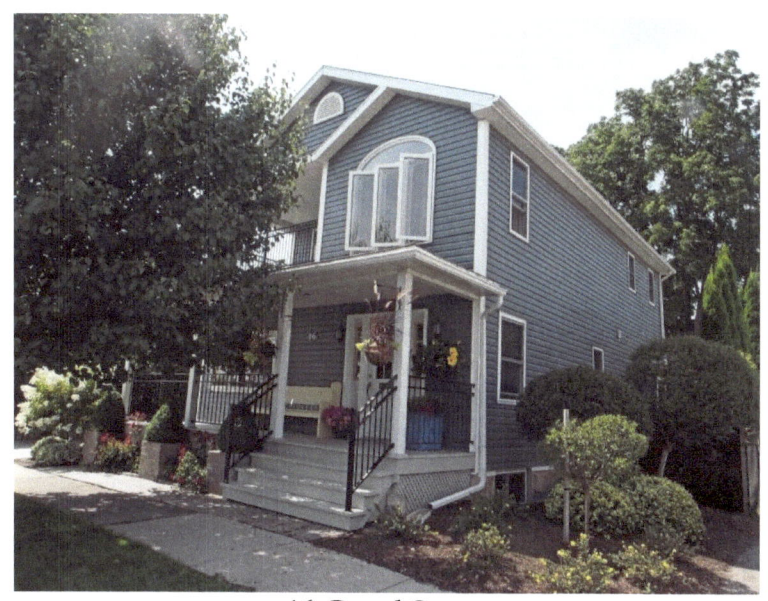

46 Canal Street

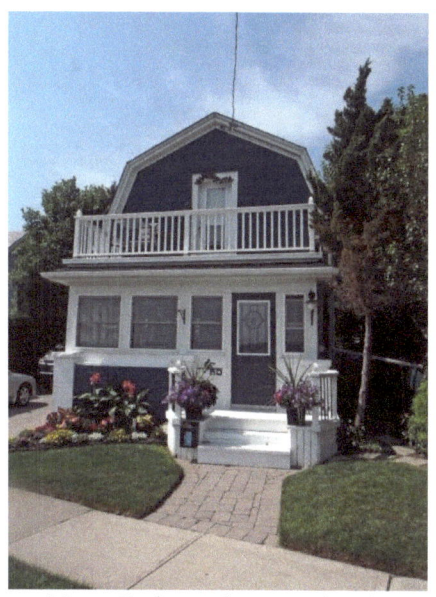

50 Canal Street – Neo-Colonial – gambrel roof, second floor balcony

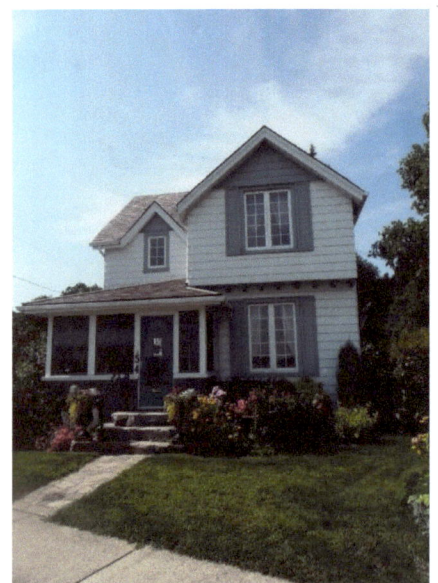 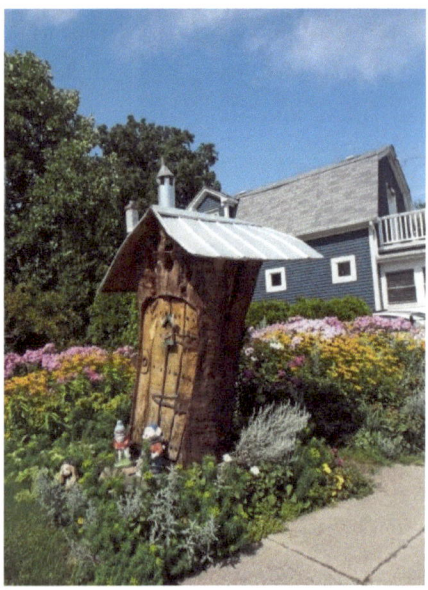

54 Canal Street

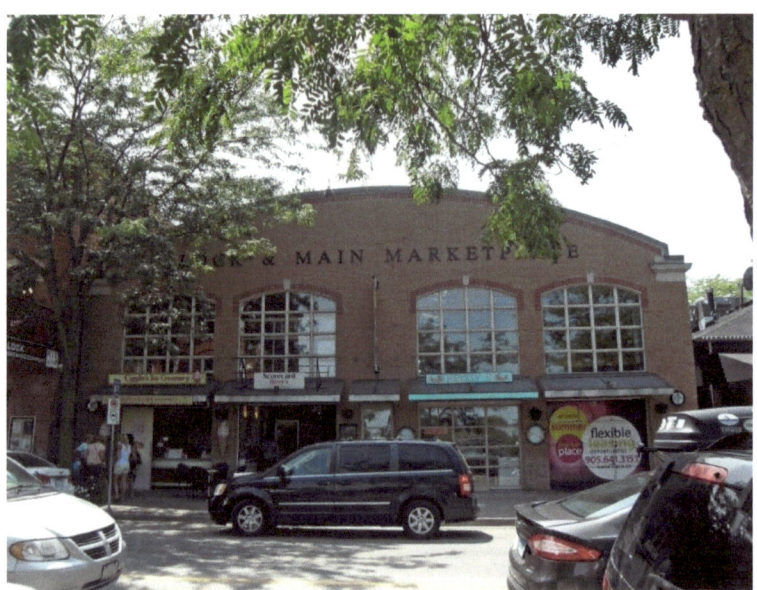

Lock and Main Marketplace

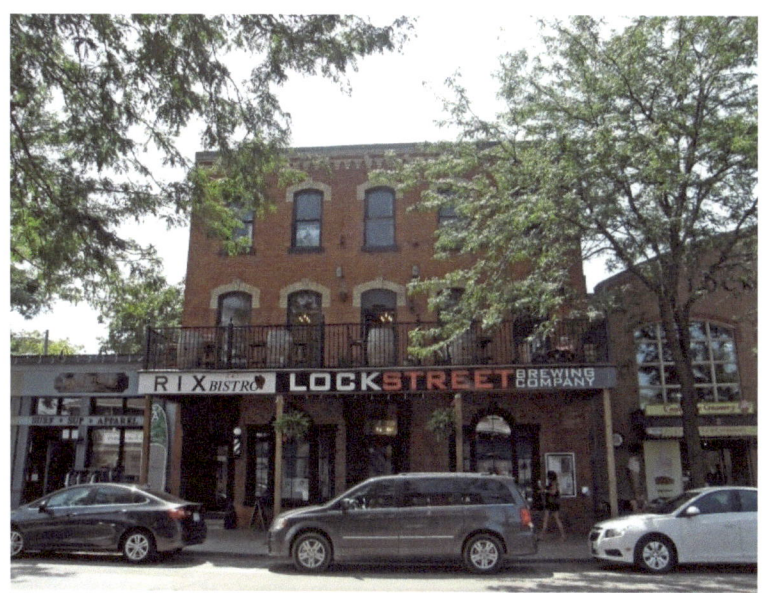

15 Lock Street - Brewing Company – voussoirs and keystones, bevelled dentil molding

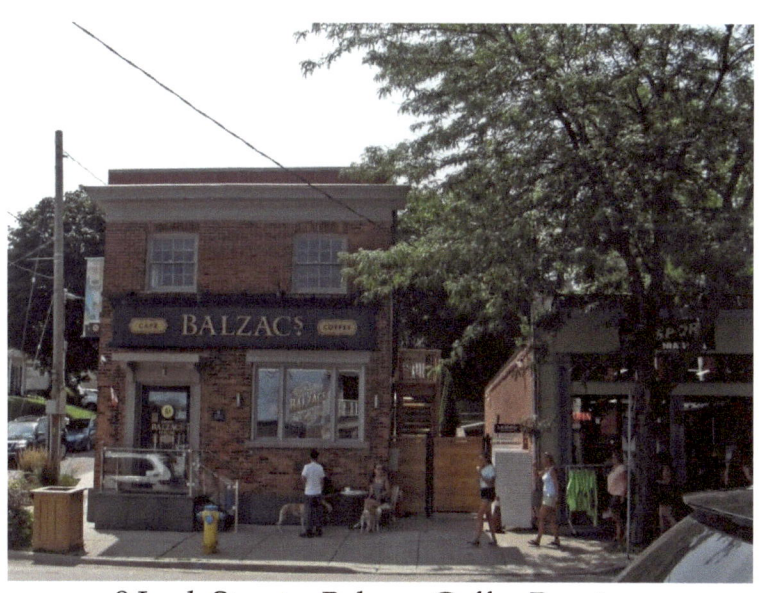

9 Lock Street – Balzacs Coffee Roasters

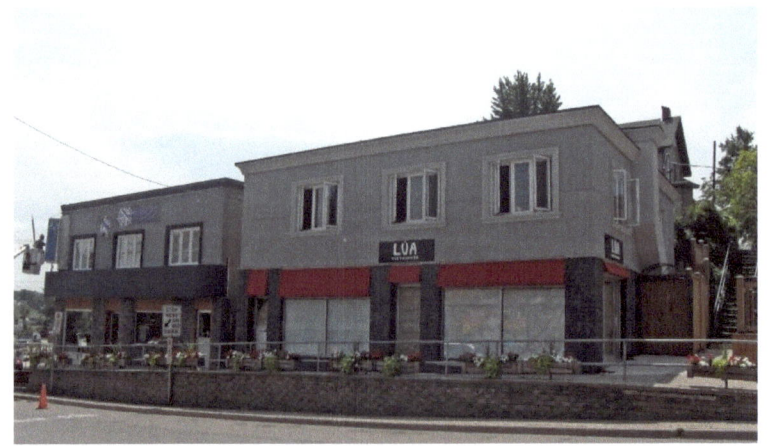

1 Lock Street – LUA Vietnamese Restaurant

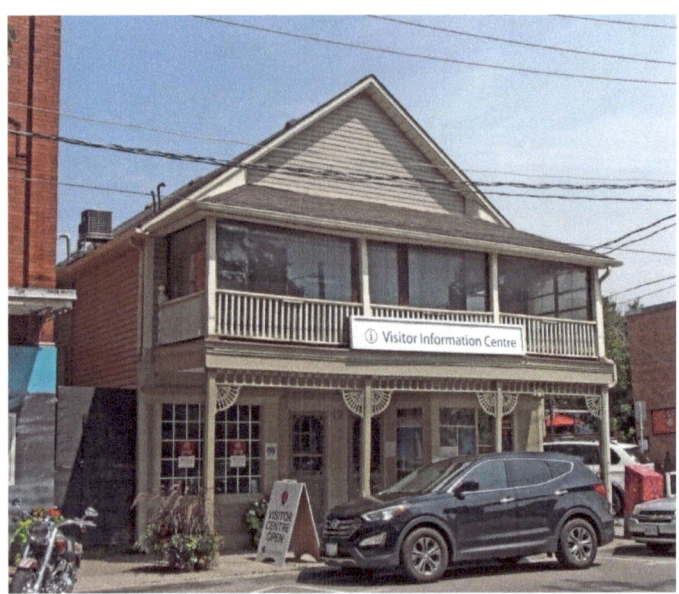

Lock Street – Visitor Information Centre

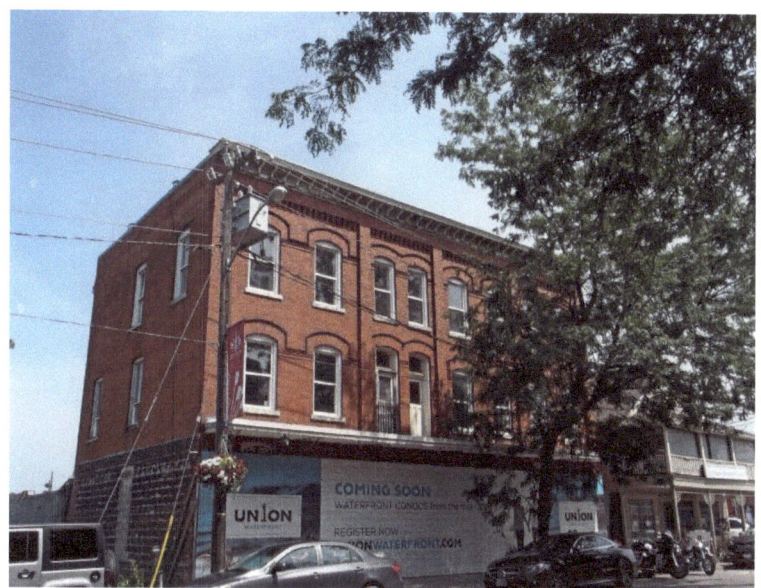

Lock Street – cornice brackets, bevelled dentil molding, pilasters, voussoirs

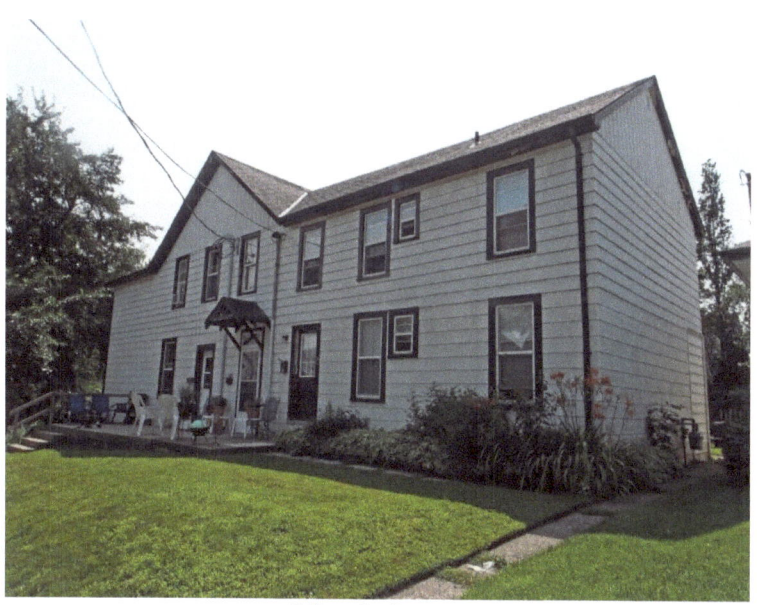

9 Lock Street

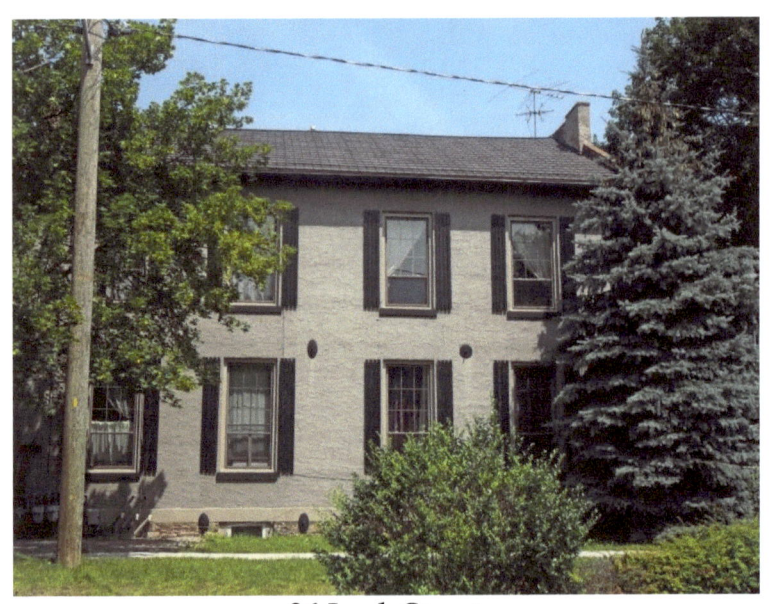

36 Lock Street

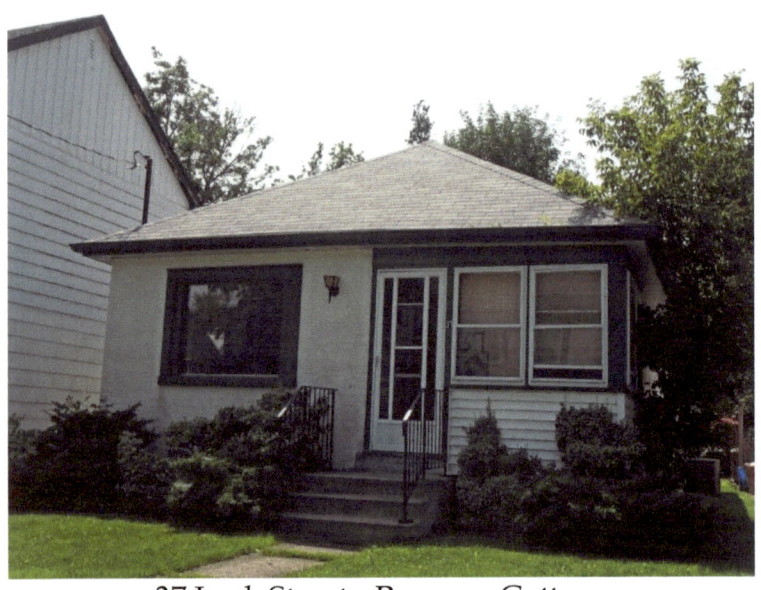

37 Lock Street - Regency Cottage

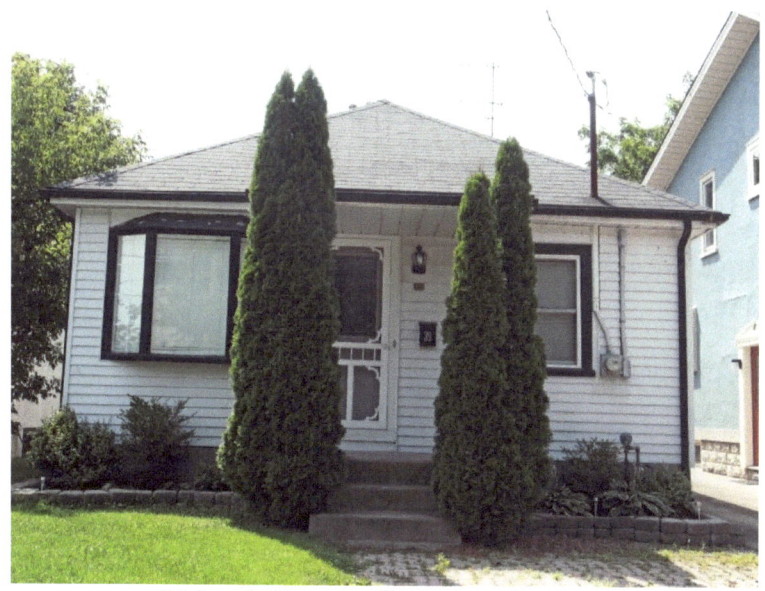

39 Lock Street - Regency Cottage

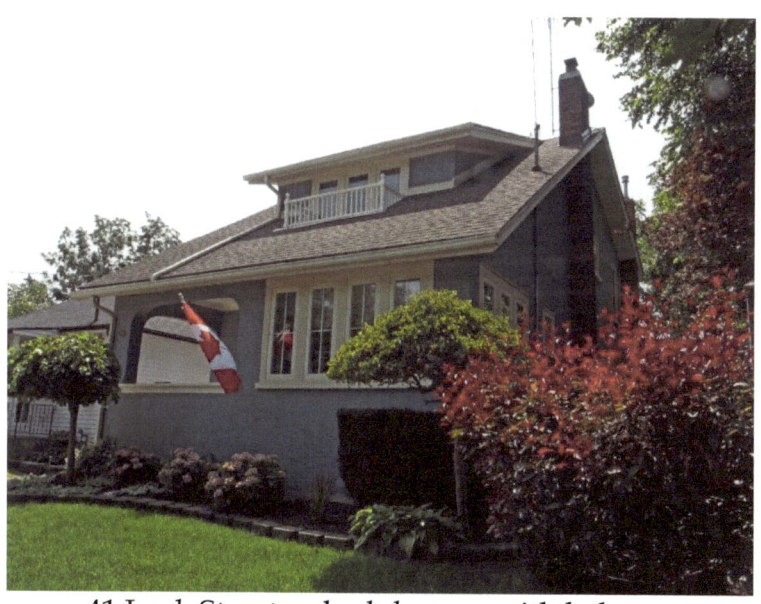

41 Lock Street – shed dormer with balcony

Architectural Terms

Bay Window: A window that projects out from a wall, in a semicircular, rectangular, or polygonal design. Used frequently in Gothic and Victorian designs. Example: 34 Main Street, Page 8	
Dentil Moulding: an even series of rectangles used as ornamental decoration in cornices. Example: 15 Lock Street, Page 61	
Dichromatic brickwork: the use of two colours of brick, tile or slate to decorate a façade. Example: 80 Main Street, Page 18	
Dormer: (French for "sleep") a gable end window that pierces through the plane of a sloping roof surface to create usable space in the top floor or attic of a building by adding headroom. Example: 40 Main Street, Page 10	
Gable: the triangular portion of a wall between the edges of a sloping roof. Example: 103 Main Street, Page 22	
Gambrel Roof: a symmetrical two-sided roof with two slopes on each side; the upper slope is positioned at a shallow angle, while the lower slope is steep. It is similar to a mansard roof, but a gambrel has vertical gable ends instead of being hipped at the four corners of the building. Example: 50 Canal Street, Page 59	
Hipped Roof: a roof where all sides slope downwards to the walls with no gables. Example: 109 Main Street, Page 24	

Keystones and Voussoirs: a voussoir is a wedge-shaped element used in building an arch. A keystone is the central stone that locks all the stones into position, allowing the arch to bear weight. Example: 15 Lock Street, Page 61	
Lancet Window: a tall, narrow window with a pointed arch at its top. Example: 92 Main Street, Page 20	
Palladian Window: a large window that is divided into three sections with the centre section larger than the two side sections and usually arched. Example: 146 Main Street, Page 32	
Pediment: a triangular section above the door or portico, usually supported by columns. The inside of the triangle is called the tympanum. Example: 103 Main Street, Page 22	
Rose Window: a circular window with ornamental tracery radiating from the centre. Example: 92 Main Street, Page 20	
Transom Window: the light above the doorway, also called a fanlight. Example: 92 Main Street, Page 20	
Verge board: also called bargeboards – hang from the projecting end of a roof and are often elaborately carved and ornamented. Example: 144 Main Street, Page 31	

Building Styles

Georgian, before 1860 – This style began with the British King Georges in the 18th century. These buildings have balanced facades around a central door, medium-pitched gable roofs, and small paned windows. Example: 27 Canal Street, Page 55	
Gothic Revival, 1830-1890 – These decorative buildings have sharply-pitched gables with highly detailed verge boards, pointed-arch window openings, and dichromatic brickwork. It is a common style in Ontario. Example: 30 Canal Street, Page 56	
Italianate, 1850-1900 – A two story rectangular building with a mild hip roof, a projecting frontispiece, and generous eaves with ornate cornice brackets was the basis of the style; often there are large sash windows, quoins, ornate detailing on the windows, belvederes and wraparound verandahs. Italianate commercial buildings often have cast iron cresting and elegant window surrounds. Example: 109 Main Street, Page 24	
Regency Cottage, 1830-1860 – This style originated in England in 1815 and spread to Ontario later in the 19th century as British officers retired to Canada. It is a modest one-storey house with a low-pitched hip roof and has a symmetrical front façade. Example: 137 Main Street, Page 30	

Saltbox: A saltbox is a building with a long, pitched roof that slopes down to the back, generally a wooden frame house. A saltbox has just one storey in the back and two stories in the front. The asymmetry of the unequal sides and the long, low rear roof line are the most distinctive features of a saltbox, which takes its name from its resemblance to a wooden lidded box in which salt was once kept. The earliest saltbox houses were created when a lean-to addition was added onto the rear of the original house extending the roof line sometimes to less than six feet from ground level. Example: 82 Main Street, Page 19	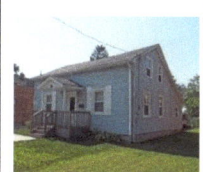
Tudor Revival – exposed timbers with stucco infill, multi-paned windows. Example: Main Street, Page 33	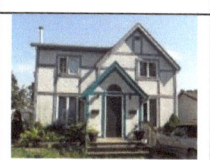
Vernacular/Traditional Mode 1638 - 1950 Influenced but not defined by a particular style, vernacular buildings are made from easily available materials and exhibit local design characteristics. Example: 112 Main Street, Page 25	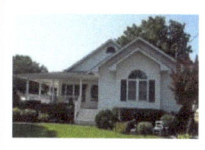

www.ingramcontent.com/pod-product-compliance
Lightning Source LLC
Chambersburg PA
CBHW041942240526
45473CB00033B/213